SERGE FAUCHEREAU

ARP

EDICIONES POLÍGRAFA, S. A.

© *1988 Ediciones Polígrafa, S. A.*
Balmes, 54 - 08007 Barcelona (Spain)

Reproduction rights:
A.D.A.G.P., Paris - L.A.R.A., S. A., Madrid
Translation by Kenneth Lyons

I.S.B.N.: 84-343-0547-X
Dep. Leg.: B. 37.974 - 1988 (Printed in Spain)

Printed in Spain by La Polígrafa, S. A.
Parets del Vallès (Barcelona)

CONTENTS

Arp in his studio. Photo: E. B. Weill.

INTRODUCTION

Arp's plastic work is extremely diversified. This diversity was fundamental to its deeper evolution: from paintings to sculptures, reliefs, collages, torn papers, wrinkled papers, drawings, woodcuts, tapestries, embroideries and works in other media. Arp also wrote prolifically throughout his life; his works include essays, reflections, memoirs, stories and, above all, poems, both in German and in French. Considering the history of painting in the first quarter of the century, this is not unusual. Quite a number of painters — ranging from Valloton to Picasso and including Kokoschka, Barlach, Vlaminck, De Chirico, Savinio and many others — wrote fiction, and several painter friends of Arp — Wassily Kandinsky, Paul Klee, Max Ernst, Kurt Schwitters and Raoul Hausmann — wrote poems. All these artists, however, with the possible exception of Alberto Savinio, created literature only after, or in addition to, their work as painters and occasionally as theorists. This was not at all the case with Arp, who in over sixty years of activity produced several volumes of poems which make him, undoubtedly in German and perhaps also in French, an important poet. And Arp himself, far from regarding writing as an ancillary occupation, confided to his friend Marcel Jean: "If I were absolutely obliged to choose between plastic work and written poetry, if I had to give up either my sculpture or my poems, I would choose to write poems" (JE, p. 25).[1] For the fact is, as we may guess from those words, that Arp considered the field of his activities to be *poetry*, the whole of poetry, whether expressed in words, in painted or drawn forms, in sculpted or cutout forms, or in any other medium. Indeed, all those who have written on Arp, including Michel Seuphor, Carola Giedion-Welcker and Herbert Read, have stressed the impossibility of dissociating plastic from written expression in the artist's work. Nor have I any intention of disagreeing. Nevertheless, in view of the framework chosen for my present monograph, we must now consider Arp's plastic work almost exclusively, passing over the written poetry. This will still give us a fairly good idea of his literary talents, for he wrote considerably on his own work, frequently evoking his life and his friends, friendship being an essential dimension of his work and one that we should be careful not to forget. In these pages, therefore, I will endeavor to let Arp speak as often as possible and to reinforce my monograph as much as I can with his own comments.

Though by now recognized as one of the great creative artists of his age, Arp occupies a less prominent position than the great stars of modern art, among whom, of course, he has a place of his own. As we shall see, indeed, Arp was hard to classify from the beginning, a situation he delighted in exaggerating throughout his professional career. There was even uncertainty regarding his name; how else could a monograph published in Germany under the title *Hans Arp* be found in the United States under that of *Jean Arp?* It seems impossible to decide — even when one knows all of the reasons for this hesitation, which greatly amused Arp himself — whether his first name should be given as Jean or Hans. Some writers try to beg the question by saying Jean/Hans Arp, or Hans/Jean Arp; and most people wisely confine themselves to saying Arp alone. All of which helps to emphasize the artist's unclassifiable character.

---

1. *Jours effeuillés: Poèmes, essais, souvenirs*, Paris: Gallimard, 1966 (henceforth as JE, followed by a page number) gathers almost all the work in prose; it is also referred to as *Unsern täglichen Traum*, Zürich: Verlag der Arche, 1955 and *Zweiklang*, Zürich: Verlag der Arche, 1960. The poems in German have appeared in three volumes of *Gesammelte Gedichte*, Zürich-Wiesbaden: Die Arche Limes, 1963-1984, as well as in an anthology, *Worttraüme und Schwarze Sterne*, Wiesbaden: Limes, 1953.

Mrs. Arp and her two sons, 1896.

Arp in front of a painting by Ritleng in Strasbourg, *c.* 1902.

THE EARLY YEARS

Hans Arp was born in Strasbourg in 1886; from the Franco-German War in 1870 to World War I, the Alsatian city was in German territory. His father spoke German and his mother, French. This was not problematic; even though German was the language spoken at school, everywhere else — particularly in the home — people spoke the Alsatian dialect. This trilingualism contributed greatly to the ease with which Arp was to move from one culture to another and with which his whole world was to develop beyond any question of narrowly defined culture. In his childhood, this did not necessarily make him a good pupil. Apart from music lessons, which he attended most assiduously along with his brother, the discipline of education seems to have been so little to his taste that in order to get him through secondary school his father, the well-to-do owner of a cigar factory, finally had to engage a private tutor.

According to his own recollections, Arp did his first sculptures, in wood, at the age of eight. During his adolescence this taste for art was strengthened, as was the passion he was never to lose for the German Romantics, preferably those from the generation of Novalis, Arnim, Brentano and Tieck. The imp-like fairy creatures capable of all sorts of metamorphoses that were to people his sculptural world many years later may have been reminiscences of his early readings of the Romantics. Arp's reading of Rimbaud and Lautréamont, of which he was always ready to talk, must have occurred considerably later, for the works of both of these authors were very hard to find at that time — even more so in German territory. In any event, the first works Arp published were poems. In the spring of 1903, the Strasbourg review *Hazweiess* published a poem in his name in the Alsatian dialect, accompanied by an illustration reproducing an impressionistic nocturnal landscape. More significantly, he published at almost the same time — signing it with the anagram "Rab" — a poem in German in *Der Stänkerer*, the ephemeral successor of another review, *Der Stürmer*, edited by René Schickelé the previous year.

As already recalled by the exhibition entitled "Paris-Berlin" at the Centre Pompidou in 1978, turn-of-the-century Strasbourg, far from being the sleepy center of an annexed territory, was the thoroughly lively scene of contacts and clashes between two cultures and the dynamic capital of a rapidly developing literary pre-expressionism. It is significant that Rilke and Döblin published their first works there. All of the men connected with *Der Stürmer* were fully aware of the specific character of Alsatian culture. In the years 1901-05, that culture was represented by the Strasbourgeois René Schickelé and Otto Flake, as well as Ernst Stadler from Colmar, among other names later to become famous (but Ivan Goll was too young to belong to that circle), and people soon became accustomed to counting young Arp among their number. He was introduced by the painter Georges Ritleng, who taught him drawing in 1902, after an unfortunate experience at the Strasbourg Arts and Crafts School. Of this period, nothing has survived but a statuette and a 1903 *Still Life* representing a vase of flowers, both of them in a severely constructed impressionistic style.

In 1904, Arp spent part of his holidays at his maternal uncle's house in Paris; but instead of leaving him there to study, his father then sent him to the Weimar School of Fine Arts, at that time directed by Henry Van de Velde, who, with the help of Count Harry Kessler, organized a number of exhibitions of new French art. Arp later recalled having been greatly impressed by an exhibition by Aristide Maillol. There he became friendly with a young painter his own age, Ivo Hauptmann (1886-1973), a great admirer of the Nabis and the Neo-Impressionists, who in 1905 painted a fine portrait of Arp that is now in the Kunsthalle in Hamburg. Arp probably was equally enthusiastic about Neo-Impressionism, for among the few works of this period to survive are some that owe much to Divisionism. I should also mention a small *Head* sculpted in 1904 and later cast in bronze from an enlarged version (1945?), though this remained an isolated work. Arp still retained his ties with Alsatia and his friends there, notably Georges Ritleng, with whom he always enjoyed arguing and painting; they collaborated on a fresco in 1905. Moreover, Schickelé published poems by him in a recently founded review; and in the anthology *Zeitgenössische Dichtung des Elsasses* (Contemporary Poetry of Alsatia), Arp's poems were given a prominent position.

Arp's links with Alsatia were to become slightly looser in 1907, for in that year his family moved to Switzerland and settled in Weggis, near Lucerne. It was also in 1907, that, thanks to a recommendation from Van de Velde, he showed in Paris for the first time at the Galerie Bernheim Jeune, along with Signac, Matisse and Van Dongen — an unexpected debut for such a young painter, though nothing much was to come of it. The following year Arp enrolled at the Académie Julian, while Ritleng was at the Académie Ranson. He does not appear to have gained much from this year of study. In Paris, however, he met several painters he was to befriend in Switzerland: Oskar Lüthy, Walter Helbing and Wilhelm Gimmi.

After his return to Weggis, Arp spent two painful years, according to his own account, trying in his loneliness to find a plastic language of his own outside the prevailing fashions. Little encouragement came his way, and Arp never forgot that of Vladimir Baranoff-Rossiné: "In 1909 I had a visit from the Russian painter Rossiné. He showed me some drawings of his in which, using colored points and lines, he had expressed his inner world in an entirely new way. They were not abstractions of landscapes, human figures or objects, as one finds in Cubist pictures. I showed him canvases which I had covered with a black web, a network of writing signs, ruins of lines and bizarre stains. This was the result of my painfully hard work over many months. The other painters, my Swiss colleagues, shrugged their shoulders, regarding what I had done as a mere collecction of unfinished sketches. Rossiné, on the contrary, was greatly impressed" (JE, p. 326). Devoured by uncertainty, Arp did not keep any of his canvases from this period. He continued his quest and, with the sculptor Fritz Huf in Lucerne, became extremely skilled in plaster modeling. Of this sculptural work, however, nothing has survived.

Arp emerged from his solitude in 1910, when the German painter Helbig, whom he had known in Paris, also came to settle in Weggis. Between them, they organized the Moderne Bund, an association of young painters who wanted to introduce modern art in Switzerland and who included Gimmi, Lüthy and Huber, among others. In December 1911, the members had their first exhibition;

their works were accompanied by those of some older Swiss artists like Hodler and C. Amiet, but there were also some Germans such as Ivo Hauptmann and, above all, a strong contingent from the Paris avant-garde, with works by Picasso, Matisse, Friesz, Chabaud, Herbin and even Gauguin, who had died some years earlier. From the invoices we learn that Arp exhibited figurative works, drawings and plaster masks.

In 1912, Arp was to receive a lasting impression from his first meeting with Wassily Kandinsky, whom he went to visit at his studio in Munich: "He gave me a very hearty welcome... Kandinsky's conversation was tender and rich, lively and witty. In his studio, words, forms and colors blended together and were transformed into fabulous, exotic works of a sort never seen before" (JE, p. 369). Kandinsky assured him, with the smiling authority of an older man, that painting and writing could go together. He showed Arp, above all, how a work should be brought to its conclusion, "naturally, like a fruit developing and ripening" (JE, p. 295). It is also quite possible that it was Kandinsky's example that was to bring him back to the nonfigurative art that he had given up three years before. Indeed Carola Giedion-Welcker has compared Arp's graphic works between 1912 and Dada to Kandinsky's drawings and doodles in *Über das Geistige in der Kunst*. Kandinsky was also to give his young visitor more specific assistance by making a little place for him in the *Blaue Reiter Almanach*, which he was publishing with Franz Marc in 1912; and in the same year, Arp was invited to take part in the *Blaue Reiter* group's second exhibition in Munich.

On Kandinsky's advice, Arp then visited Klee. The Moderne Bund's second exhibition was presenting not only painters it had already introduced, but also the *Blaue Reiter* group (Kandinsky, Marc, Klee, Gabriele Münter) and their friends (Robert Delaunay, Henri le Fauconnier). In 1913 the Moderne Bund was to exhibit in Berlin again at the Galerie Der Sturm, that stronghold of Expressionism, and in several other German cities. In the same year, with his friend Lucien Neitzel,a former classmate at school in Strasbourg, Arp published for Schickelé's review *Die Weissen Blätter* in Leipzig *La nouvelle peinture française*, a selection of reproductions of works by Matisse, Derain, Picasso, Van Dongen and the Douanier Rousseau. With work published in *Der Sturm*, and participating from now on in its exhibitions, Arp was by now well launched on his career. And yet, what remains today of his work of that period? Hardly anything, because he himself destroyed the works he created before World War I. Arp was always to be a great destroyer of his own works once they no longer pleased him; hence the legend vouched for by some of his friends of an Arp born spontaneously as an artist ("At the start of his career as an artist we do not find any marked influence from earlier schools," Gabrielle Buffet tells us). To help us form an idea of this immediately pre-war period in Arp's work, all we have are some reproductions in reviews of the day, some drawings and a very small number of canvases saved from destruction by his brother or by one or another of his friends. While some of the characters drawn during the Weimar period had rather sinuous outlines, those of the *Blaue Reiter* period are still further simplified, reduced to outline alone — as in the work of several Expressionists and of Matisse. Particularly attractive are three or four paintings of bathers done in 1912 and 1913, in which the influence of the Fauvist and Cubist simplifications is evident. An example of this is the 1912 *Three Women*, described by Michel Seuphor as "a large grisaille representing three summarily treated nudes, somewhat in the style of Matisse, but more heavily, announcing the sculptor rather than the painter." It was not so much the color that interested Arp, but the construction of three massive bodies, looking as if they had been cut by a hatchet, the hands and faces barely marked, the forms represented by shadowy traces and without any attempt at softness or roundness. Compared with Cézanne's *Bathers*, or with the Fauvist bathers of Matisse, Derain, or, later on, Vlaminck, they are more barbaric and, ultimately, closer to the Expressionist painting of *Die Brücke* or the "Black" period of Cubism (1907-08): Picasso's *Les demoiselles d'Avignon, La fermière* or *La driade*, or Braque's *Large Nude*, for instance. A desire for incompletion and an imprecision of design that are foreign to Cubism are still to be found in these works: the occasional absence of hands at the end of arms, inaccuracies in the attachment of members to the body, schematic faces that are in effect nonexistent on enormous cylindrical necks. It is as if the spontaneity that was to prevail in Dada were already in effect here.

1914-1915

1914 was destined to be a decisive year in the orientation of the life and work of Arp. The first milestone was his encounter with Max Ernst, with whom he would be linked in an important friendship. With Ernst, he met the group of Rhenish Expressionists of which August Macke was a member and through whom he saw the works of the *Blaue Reiter*. In Ernst, Arp saw his own anticonformism expressed in painting as well as in writing. Unfortunately, they did not have the time to collaborate, since the declaration of war took them by surprise and Ernst had to take up the army uniform. In principle German citizens, the Arp brothers were draftable; they made straight for Paris.

Arp installed himself in Montmartre, where he was to spend nine difficult but stimulating months. The difficulty stemmed from a lack of resources in day-to-day life; but this was happily compensated by the amicable stimulation he received from the painters and poets whom he met, including the Delaunays, Apollinaire, Max Jacob, Picasso, Herbin, Modigliani and Viking Eggeling. He was to establish long-lasting friendships with Eggeling, whom he was to meet again in Zurich; Herbin, with whom he would organize "Abstraction-Création" twenty years later; and Sonia and Robert Delaunay, who were to be friends for life. The artists helped each other with the initiative of Marie Vassilieff: "That woman organized in her two shops a cafeteria where the artists could eat every evening for little money" (JE, p. 307). The Alsatian solidarity could still be counted upon. René Schwaller, a friend from childhood and a fellow student in the lycée in Strasbourg, was to ask Arp to do the decoration of the theosophical institute he had founded in connection with the magazine *Le Théosophe*. Arp was not particularly enthusiastic about

Arp in Paris in front of his collages for the Theosophic Institute, 1914.

theosophy, which was too intellectual a speculation for his temperament; nevertheless, it was in the air of the period and if Arp did not share the passionate interest that Mondrian had in it, he at least knew the theosophy of Kandinsky's *On the Spiritual in Art*. In 1914, following a suggestion by René Schwaller, he had already completed a set of drawings to illustrate the *Bhagavad-Gita*, but it was with particular spirit that he undertook the decoration of the Theosophical Institute, since this was to be done with his first collages. He was to say about them: "Actually, it was in Paris in 1914 that I did my first collages, for an occultist friend. They where mysterious porticos which were supposed to replace mural paintings and which evoked the structure of palm branches or fishbones" (JE, p. 430). These comments and some rare photographs of the period give something of an idea of what these works, which have since disappeared, were like and demonstrate that they depended to a great extent on the effects of symmetry. Their importance is that they are the first manifestation of an interest in symmetry that was to reappear several times along the course of Arp's career, from wooden carvings of the Dada period to certain collages and sculptures of the 'sixties.

The ostensible use of symmetry was a gesture of independence from the current esthetic, Cubism, and even more so from all figurative art, Fauvist or Expressionist. Arp was well aware of it: "They were very different from the Cubist *papiers collés*. All I have left of these collages are the little photographs taken by my brother. Through Herbin's intermediary, who lived not far away, in the Place Ravignan, in Bateau-Lavoir, I met Léonce Rosenberg, of the L'Effort Gallery, at 19 Beaune Street. He was interested in my collages and spoke vaguely about a contract. Later events did away with these indefinite plans. These collages were static symmetrical constructions, porticos with pathetic vegetation, the gateway to the realm of dreams. They were done with colored paper in black, orange or blue dye plates. Although Cubist painting interested me very much, not a trace of their influence was to be found in my collages" (JE, p. 420). Another way of distancing himself from Cubism was to practice a certain disorder. "He immediately eliminates," writes Gabrielle Buffet, "the concern for good design, for classical good taste, which Cubism still embraces." There still exist, on the other hand, several examples of this second type of collage that escaped destruction by their author. They differ surprisingly from the large Cubist collages by Picasso, Braque, Gris or Laurens. An example is the *Composition Abstraite* (Abstract Composition) of 1915. There is not a trace of abstract naturalism in it, no signs referring back to a visible reality. The work and its components refer only to themselves: a paper doily, placed almost on a diagonal, which overlaps other papers; a piece of tissue with a leaf and flower pattern; and the smashed corner of a cardboard box. All of this is neither decorative nor figurative, arranged as if according to the laws of chance. In effect, the disparity and the sense of "rubbish" that the materials communicate in a collage like this one recall the Mertz montages that Kurt Schwitters was about to undertake.

Apart from Cubism, then, there was another strong current that Arp had to take into account: Futurism. The previous year in Berlin he saw the work of the Italian Futurists, and in Paris he met one of them, Gino Severini, whom he encountered either with Apollinaire or with Modigliani. Futurism, like Cubism, is an esthetic based on visual reality, and Arp disapproved of this. On the other hand, Futurism has an interest in plastic dynamism which Arp found as rich in possibilities as its opposite, staticism and strict symmetry. There still exists a drawing in India ink and gouache from 1915, curiously entitled *Crucifixion*, in which there is not a trace of representation (or may a head crowned with thorns be found in it?). More than from a religious motif, the origin of this title stems from the play of diagonal lines that intersect and animate the work, from the sharp angles that stamp it with an ascending movement, as in certain works the Italian Prampolini was to exute in this period or slightly afterwards. In any case, Arp liked this *Crucifixion* enough to make a tapestry of it. Indeed, in 1915 he developed an interest in this new means of expression, as well as in embroidery and other techniques habitually repudiated by the fine arts as being too artisanal.

But in 1915, as the routine of the war became entrenched, Arp's situation grew uncomfortable: even though he had opted for France, he was still a German citizen. Since he had the good sense not to manifest his patriotic sentiments, he had no other choice than to move to neutral territory. He left for Switzerland in 1915. In Zurich, Arp found a cosmopolitan atmosphere just like that of Paris. He was welcomed by Arthur Segal, of Rumanian origin, and by Adya and Otto van Rees, a Dutch artist couple with whom he was later to engage in a fruitful collaboration.

In 1915, Arp and Otto van Rees collaborated on an abstract fresco in the entrance hall of the Pestalozzi School in Zurich. It consists of interwoven geometric motifs, without depth, in some ways similar to those of *Crucifixion*. In November of that year, Arp did an exhibition in the Tanner Gallery in Zurich with the van Reeses: "This show, in which Otto van Rees and A.C. van Rees-Dutilh also took part, was largely composed of tapestries, embroidery, and collages.... The essential characteristic of this show was the search by the artists, who were tired of oil painting, for new materials" (JE, p. 355). It was in effect the first time that Arp manifested in public his disenchantment with easel painting. In the catalogue of the show, he made one of his first professions of faith. Once expressed, it seemed so fundamental to him that he would quote it several times during the course of

his life: "These works are constructed with lines, with surfaces, with shapes, with colors which try to attain, beyond the merely human, the infinite and the eternal. They negate our egoism.... The hands of our brothers, instead of serving us as if they were our own, have become the hands of the enemy. Celebrity and the masterpiece have replaced anonymity; wisdom is dead.... To reproduce is to imitate, to play the comedy, to dance on the tightrope" (JE, pp. 183 and 106). Here, Arp introduced ideas that he took permanently to heart and to which he would refer often. He denounced the anthropocentrism that causes man to see himself not as an element among so many others in nature, but rather as at the center of nature itself. All of art is influenced by this attitude: man likes to imagine himself for himself and copy nature at will, as if he himself had created it. Nonrepresentative art should eliminate man and his maniacal individualism. Therefore, art should be anonymous; artists should help one another instead of competing; and they should even do work in common. "These paintings, these sculptures — these objects — should remain anonymous, in the great workshop of nature, like the clouds, the mountains, the seas, the animals, and man himself. Yes! Man should go back to nature! Artists should work together like the artists of the Middles Ages. In 1915, O. van Rees, A.C. van Rees, Freundlich, S. Taeuber and I myself made an attempt of this sort" (JE, p. 183). Doesn't Tzara speak of Dada as an anonymous collective?

These ideas were the result of a maturing of Arp's esthetic. If the exhibition of 1915 was "the main event of his life," the reason lies elsewhere: "It was there I met Sophie Taeuber for the first time" (JE, p. 355). From then on, he would never stop emphasizing the ways in which she influenced him, or the merits of the woman, the artist with whom he would soon be sharing life: "It was Sophie who, by the example of her work and her life, both of them bathed in clarity, showed me the right way. In her world, the high and the low, the light and the dark, the eternal and the ephemeral, are balanced in perfect equilibrium" (*Unsern täglichen Traum*, p. 76). Born in Devos in 1889, Sophie Taeuber was slightly more than two years older than Arp. At the time at which they met, she taught applied arts and studied dance at the Laban School while developing her own work as an artist. Sufficiently confident in her own abilities to be both modest and self-assured, she was to be the ideal artistic partner for Arp. Hans Richter said jokingly that "she was as much the discovery of Arp as Arp was her own." It is very possible that Arp's example pushed her more and more to the plastic arts. He himself wrote that at the beginning, "during a certain period, dance was her main activity, she preferred it to her other artistic activities" (JE, p. 358); this was to have an impact on Dada events and the important part that dance was to play in them.

From the time they met, Arp and Taeuber undertook a collaboration that was to last their entire lives. Arp was certainly impressed by the self-assurance of the young artist for whom the problem of representation was not even to be posed; she was already elaborating the compositions of characteristic rectangles (without knowing that Mondrian, Itten and Klee were then working on these same chromatic figures, from another frame of mind). "Already in 1915, Sophie Taeuber divides the surface of her aquarelles into squares and rectangles which she then

11

juxtaposes horizontally and perpendicularly. She constructs them as if they were masonry work. The colors are luminous, ranging from the rawest yellow to deep red or blue" (JE, p. 288). Finally, and above all, Sophie Taeuber shared Arp's taste for anything other than traditional work with oil paint. During all of the war years, they were to dedicate themselves to what are customarily called the applied arts, perhaps with an absurdly pejorative nuance that Arp would denounce on several occasions. "Sophie Taeuber and I had decided to renounce completely the use of oil colors in our compositions. We wanted to avoid any references to the paintings which seemed to us characteristic of a pretentious and ostentatious world. In 1916, Sophie Taeuber and I began to work together on large compositions in fabric and paper. I embroidered with Sophie Taeuber's help a series of vertical and horizontal configurations.... In the years during which we worked exclusively with new materials, I made embroidery and configurations in paper and in fabric, and it affected us like a sort of purification, like spiritual exercises, so that finally we rediscovered painting in its original state of purity" (JE, pp. 356 and 358). It was thus a period in which there appeared a certain number of pieces executed in collaboration — in duo, as Arp preferred to say. There would be many others — in the 'twenties, working at the Aubette in Strasbourg; in the 'thirties in Meudon, during the Second World War; and even, as we will see, after Taeuber's death — in which the respective contributions of one or the other are impossible to identify, helping them to achieve their desire to truly work in common.

THE BIRTH OF DADA

It was to be a great effort in teamwork, a great revolutionary adventure that would occupy Arp and Taeuber for four or five years: Dada, to which they would commit themselves with all of their abilities, with enthusiasm and without second thoughts. The origins of the bizarre and derisive name, "Dada", and whose idea it really was are unknown. The best account, which is probably false, is that Tzara invented it by opening the dictionary at random. On the other hand, it is known exactly how and with whom Dada had its debut. It all began with the German Hugo Ball (1886-1927), a scriptwriting student of Max Reinhardt's, a philosopher and renegade poet of the Expressionist review *Die Aktion*. After having been declared unfit for military service, Ball installed himself in Zurich with his friend Emmy Hennings, a singer and comedienne.

In a Europe put to fire and the sword, Switzerland was a peaceful oasis where the draft dodgers escaping the war and anyone else who thought he had something better to do could rendezvous. René Schickelé moved his review *Die Wiessen Blätter* to Bern. In Geneva, Romain Rolland, Pierre-Jean Jouve, Frans Masereel, Henri Guilbeaux and an entire group of intellectuals wanted "to rise above the melée." (Their relations with Dada were to become strained.) Zurich was the inevitable center, frequented by the most diverse personalities, from Lenin to James Joyce. Expressionist painters and writers from Germany were

Julie Ackermann, Arp and Janco, Zurich, 1916-1918.

particularly numerous: Jawlenski and Marianne von Werefkin of the *Blaue Reiter* (Kandinsky was to stop by only briefly before going back to Russia), Else Lasker-Schüler, Ferdinand Hardekopf, Albert Ehrenstein, Max Oppenheimer and Leonhard Frank took an active part in Dada. Among them, of course, was Hugo Ball, who rented a tavern in the Spiegelgasse in Zurich at the beginning of 1916 to organize an artist's cabaret. A brief communiqué announced its opening in the newspapers: "Cabaret Voltaire. Under this name, a company of young artists and writers has been organized with the objective of creating a center for artistic activities. The opening plans include daily sessions with musical programs and poetry readings by the artists present in the audience. All young artists of Zurich, of all tendencies, are invited to lend their support and contribute their ideas." Its success was immediate. Above all, Ball had the chance to surround himself very quickly with those who were to unflaggingly animate his cabaret. In his journal *Die Flucht aus der Zeit*, he recounts the opening of the Cabaret Voltaire: "The hall was packed; there were many who were not able to find a seat! Toward six in the evening, when we were still busy tacking up Futurist posters, a group of four men with an oriental air made their entry; they made a good many polite reverences, and then introduced themselves: the painter Marcel Janco, Tristan Tzara, Georges Janco and a fourth character whose name escapes me. By chance, Arp was also there, and not many words were needed before they began to understand each other. Soon the noble *Archangels* by Janco were hanging amidst the other beautiful things, and that same evening Tzara read verses in an old style which he fished good-humoredly from his jacket pockets." Tzara, Janco, Arp; only the poet Richard Huelsenbeck was missing, and he would arrive from Germany six days later. Ball's team would then be complete.

Ball shared Arp's admiration for Kandinsky. He therefore believed in the necessary fusion of all the arts; in the Cabaret Voltaire, there were art shows, instrumental performances, singing, dancing, theater, recitals, poetry readings; there was shouting, too, and the public was willingly shaken out of its normal habits. German was spoken to the same extent as French, and even Russian and Rumanian could be heard. Debussy and Scriabine were placed side by side with light-hearted songs, as were the most recent French poets with the Expressionists of Berlin, or even with Chekhov. The tone became bolder, and the desire to push the audience a bit further became evident. If Tzara and Huelsenbeck were the most boisterous ringleaders, the painters Janco and Arp were no less active: Janco's masks caused a sensation, and even though Arp defended abstract art on April 13, it was equally significant to watch him interpret a scene from Alfred Jarry's *Ubu Roi* on April 14: Jarry's devastating humor was destined to seduce him. For Arp, humor was the antidote to the Cubist order; it was even more a reaction against the Expressionist pathos, a refusal to be banished to the tragic, which the historical circumstances so easily evoked. On the first of March of that year, Ball recorded a valuable perspective on Arp's position: "Arp takes a position against the turgidity of the gods of painting — the Expressionists. Marc's bulls seemed too fat to him; the cosmogonies, the crazed fixed stars by Baumann and Meidner reminded him of the stars by Bölsche and Carus. He would have liked things to be in a stricter order, less arbitrary, less overflowing with color and poetry. He suggested plane geometry instead of twilights and apocalypses in painting. If he tends toward simplicity, it is because he thinks of the first abstract outline, which does not ignore complications, but which is not placated by them. It is necessary to eliminate sentiment and the debate which it implies on the canvas. That explains his tendency toward circles and cubes with absolutely clean lines. He is in favor of the use of simple colors (preferably printed ones), of color paper, of fabric.... If I understand him correctly, richness gives him less than simplicity." Arp was never to abandon these ideas, even after Dada.

At the beginning of June, the Almanac *Cabaret Voltaire* appeared under the direction of Ball. The entire team collaborated on it (both in German and in French), along with several "outside" personalities for whom the team felt sympathy: Apollinaire, Cendrars, J. van Hoddis, Kandinsky, Marinetti and Picasso. Ball defined its activity and announced the next step (in somewhat rough French): "The goal is to remember that there are, above and beyond the war and patriotism, independent men who live according to other ideals. The intention of the artists assembled here is to publish an international review. The review will appear in Zurich and will be called 'Dada' Dada Dada Dada Dada." The activities of the group of friends began again just as successfully, all the more so because some new arrivals were about to join: the painters Hans Richter and Christian Schad, for example, and the poet Walter Serner. The tone became even more virulent because the war continued, more deadly than ever. In his *Manifeste de monsieur Antipyrine*, read in July of 1916, Tzara asserts: "We exteriorize facility, we search for the main essence" and "Art is not serious, I assure you." Facility, as Tzara said, and clean simplicity, in Arp's words, appear frequently in the texts and illustrations of the publications of the Dada collection. In the first issue of the review *Dada* and in the *Phantastische Gebete* (1916) by Huelsenbeck, we notice drawings and wood engravings that are perfectly symmetrical, organized around a vertical axis like the squares of a mysterious chess game, or like totems, large nonfigurative fetishes (it was in this period

that Tzara and Huelsenbeck were enthusiastic about African art).

In the second issue of *Dada* in 1917, Tzara pays tribute to his friend and to his symmetrical creations:

H. Arp
Symmetry
flower of meeting at midnight
where vertigo and bird turn into quietness of halo
and hops grow
the flower becomes crystal or scarab magnet star
a will to lead a simple life

(transl. S. Fauchereau)

By this time, Arp and Taeuber had created a series of objects with extremely purified lines, including tapestries, table mats and wooden powder compacts. The most characteristic is certainly *Amphora* (1916). Executed in wood turned by machine and then painted, it is actually the placement of two chalices side by side; since the neck of the resulting amphora is almost as large as the base, both vertical and horizontal symmetry are invoked.

After a year of existence, and ceding to the criticisms of the neighbors, the Cabaret Voltaire was forced to close. But the Dada activities were begun again immediately, on March 18, 1917, in another space, the Corray Gallery; the activities consisted mainly of art exhibitions and dance shows, the latter due to a regular collaboration with the dancers of the Laban School, one of whom was Sophie Taeuber (on March 29, she executed an "abstract dance" to a poem by Ball, with a mask by Arp, according to an entry in Ball's journal). But at the end of May, Ball retired definitively to the country, perhaps to be able to dedicate himself to his mystical reflections and philosophizing though also perhaps because a tendency toward anarchistic revolt was growing among his friends (but had not he himself written a book about Bakunin?) which Tzara was to synthesize in his *Dada Manifesto 1918*. The departure of Ball, after that of Huelsenbeck, marked a turning point in the history of Dada that Richter described retrospectively: "As long as the lean silhouette of Ball was present in the Dada circles of Zurich, the anti-art movement did not adopt an anarchistic form. Of course, Arp, Janco, and I agreed with the latest calls for relaxation of standards by Serner and Tzara, but only as a way to obtain new and exceptional arms to destroy the depraved and superfluous past, to protect ourselves against the petit bourgeoisie, and to dig the ditch which would separate us from banality (even in ourselves)." The "Dada disgust" which Tzara discusses was felt by all of his companions. It was not only disgust with conventional art, but also with the society of which the war gave a frightful image, particularly in the terrible year of 1917. Arp was to say: "In Zurich, disinterested in the slaughtering of the World War, we devoted ourselves to the fine arts. While the thunder of battle sounded in the distance, we stuck together, we recited, we versified, we sang of all of our souls. We were looking for an elementary art which should, we thought, save man from the furious folly of the times. We aspired to a new order which could reestablish equilibrium between heaven and hell" (JE, p. 306). This is far from being the attitude of an esthete or an ostrich who averts his face. The anarchism of which Dada is accused has its roots in this disgust. I have shown elsewhere ("Expressionnisme, dada, surréalisme," *Denoël*, vol. 2, Paris, 1976) how Tzara

Otto Flake, Arp and Tzara, Zurich, c. 1917.

going to serve as a witness, from which originated such a series of denials and counter-denials that no one knew what to think about the fictitious duel or whether the two opponents would mutually capitulate. This transcends the merely anecdotal in that Dada was building itself into a system and that once it had gained Paris and Berlin, it would not be forgotten. Most surprising of all is that apart from the ill humor that Dada provoked (and the resulting lack of success of its works in the general public), sympathizers were constantly being attracted to the movement from the ranks of artists who did not belong to it: Alsatian writers like Neitzel or Otto Flake, recruited by Arp, Jawlensky, Eggeling or even by a local "elder brother," Augusto Giacometti, a painter of some renown whose abstract and anticonformist work paralleled that of the Dadaists.

THE DADAIST ŒUVRE

If Dada was the fundamental period of Arp's artistic career, it was because an extremely fertile process took place during so much feverish activity. In this period, Arp definitely marked out the foundations of his art; and even if he had not yet discovered all of the techniques that he would later use, at least the directions and the general principles were set.

Richter has said that the Dadaists "took laughing seriously." It was, in effect, their main weapon; and Tzara's laugh was formidable. Arp's laugh was more interior than those of his companions, and the effectiveness of his smile has been applauded by some of the greatest masters of humor. In Tzara's words, "Let's rejoice, there's still time, before art sells itself like diplomas for the Cubist pawns, Futurists or purists, these leeches of organized stupidity, these damned nuisances of self-contentment and of stinking, scientific vanity. I salute you, Arp, you slight smile of the sea rains." A quarter of a century later, when Dada had already accomplished its work, Marcel Duchamp would recognize one of its constants: "Arp has shown the importance of the smile in the struggle against the sophisticated theories of the epoch." Arp always found artistic poses and grandiose opinions ridiculous: "In the good times of Dada, we detested polished works, the distracted air of spiritual struggle, the titans, and we rejected them with all our being" (Preface to *Wortträume und schwarze Sterne*). Arp summed up the objectives of Dada in a sentence that echoes the *Dada Manifesto 1918:* "We rejected all copying or description to allow the Elementary and the Spontaneous to react in total freedom" (JE, p. 307). One recognizes in these words the main principles of Dada to which Arp would always remain faithful. At the height of his anger with traditional art, Arp could never imagine a better antidote than to integrate himself as quickly as possible with nature and to become himself another one of its elements. Throughout his career, Arp had often repeated, unchanged, the following phrases: "Dada has given the Venus de Milo a clyster and has allowed Laocoön and his sons to rest awhile, after thousands of years of struggle with the good sausage Python. The philosophers are of less use to Dada than an old

had copied from the *Catéchisme révolutionnaire* attributed to Bakunin in his *Dada Manifesto 1918*. Now, even though Arp was opposed to all violence, one must still be struck by the large number of formulas he ratified and that he would cite from time to time:

> *After the carnage, we are left with hope for a purified humanity.*
>
> • *We do not recognize any theory. We have had enough of Cubist and Futurist academies: laboratories of formal ideas. Does one make art to earn money and caress the nice bourgeois?*
>
> • *I destroy the compartments of the brain and those of social organization: to demoralize everywhere, and the hand of heaven should strike in hell, the eyes of hell in heaven, to reestablish the fertile wheel of a universal circus in the real powers and the fantasy of each individual.*
>
> • *DADA SPONTANEITY*
>
> • *Without goal or design, without organization.*
>
> • *Absolute, indisputable belief in each god produced immediately by spontaneity: Dada.*

During the war years, the Dadaists were to systematically go against the grain of "the nice bourgeois." Arp was to continue for a long time to "accuse bourgeois art of sheer madness" (JE, p. 322). Not content with shocking those who attended their events, they bothered them in their daily lives by deliberately spreading false news: for example, they published in several newspapers that the Dada chiefs, Tzara and Arp, were going to fight a duel and that a local person of note was toothbrush, and it leaves them on the scrap heap for the great leaders of the world. Dada denounces the infernal ruses of the official vocabulary of wisdom. Dada is for the sense-less, which does not mean nonsense. Dada is without sense, like nature. Dada is for nature against art. Dada is direct like nature. Dada is for infinite sense and for defined means'' (JE, pp. 63, 76 and 312). With this verbal attack against two of the most celebrated works in the history of sculpture, the *Venus* of the Louvre and the *Laocoön* of the Vatican, Arp expresses what is probably his most specific contribution to Dada, as well as one of his personal constants: the denunciation of the anthropocentrism of man and his art. "Since the time of the cavemen, man has glorified himself, has made himself divine, and his monstrous vanity has caused human catastrophe. Art has collaborated in this false development. I find this conception of art which has sustained man's vanity to be loathsome'' (JE, p. 315). Dada is a child of war, and we see in such comments how Arp established a direct cause and effect between the vanity of man as manifested through his art, where he takes pleasure in representing his predominance, and the rivalries and massacres that signal its existence. The Dadaists asked themselves if in changing art, it would not also be possible to change somewhat the behavior of man himself: "I wanted," wrote Arp, "to find another order, another value for man in nature. He should no longer be the measure of all things, nor should everything be compared to him, but, on the contrary, all things, and man as well, should be like nature, without measure. I wanted to create new appearances, to extract new forms

Arp and Sophie Taeuber, Zurich, 1918.

from man. This is made clear in my *objets* from 1917'' (JE, p. 311).

By *objets*, Arp was not referring so much to sculptures (he had destroyed those that he had done in 1915) as to forms that surfaced first in the graphic research to which he dedicated himself in 1917, after having abandoned the effects of symmetry for a time: "I drew with a brush and India ink broken branches, roots, grass, and stones which the lake had thrown up on the shore. Finally, I simplified these forms and united their essence in moving ovals, symbols of metamorphosis and of development of bodies'' (JE, p. 357). This period from 1917-20 was to mark a high point in Arp's graphic work and to affirm the importance of black and white in his work. When Camille Bryen pointed this out to him in 1955, he replied: "I use very little red. I use blue, yellow, a little green, but especially, as you say, black, white and gray. There is a certain need in me for communication with human beings. Black and white is writing,'' (JE, p. 432). Thus, what should be seen in the ink drawings and wood engravings that punctuate the Dada reviews (*Dada, Der Zeltweg*) are *calligraphies without sense*, which nevertheless do not exclude communication. These signs, which hail us, are simple drawings; for example, three blots included over a hollowed-out blot, or black lines and forms ajouréed with white. The two series of wood engravings for *Twenty-five Poems* (1918) and *Cinema Calendar of the Abstract Heart Houses* (1920) by Tzara present a complete display of forms, from irregular black-and-white rosettes — navel forms with which Arp will never cease to play — to the placement of open and closed forms that are the enemy of geometrical regularity. After the first absolutely illegible calligraphies, Arp would not trouble himself if the randomness of the blots — and not the will of the person drawing them — would suggest to the imagination a key, dumbbells, a two-footed bottle, or anything that fantasy itself would be pleased to discern. Arp would not deprive himself, either, of inventing fantastic titles suggested by these forms (see *Bird Mask*, 1917). Thus, these works by Arp, created *automatically* by movements of the hand and not by decisions of the intellect, are closer to Rorschach inkblots than to Kandinsky's wood and abstract designs, to which they have been related. Richter has left us a good description of the frenzy of spontaneous creation that animated Arp: "In his Zeltweg studio, collages piled up beside drawings. I passed by there one morning, and I watched for a while how coleopteres, plants, fragments of characters, violins, and stars, serpents, or even ears were born from his hands. When I went back to collect him at midday, the table was covered with pages full of Arpesque vegetation. I could not understand how, with no qualms and with a serene conscience, he could create such a confusion in so short a time. 'What do you want?' he asked me. It grows like the toenails on the feet. I have to cut them and they still grow." This automatism, which did not wait for Surrealism to reveal itself as being important, also manifests itself in the poems that Arp wrote simultaneously and that he would assemble in *Die Wolkenpumpe* (1920), or those he would compose with Tzara and Serner. The three compose in turn their roles on paper, without preconceived ideas, everything falling by chance from their pens, happily mixing languages; here, by Arp, Serner and Tzara is an extract from *Institut Montgolfier pour l'entretien de la beauté:*

The randomness that Dada stresses so much also manifests itself in the collages that Arp, possibly in collaboration with Taeuber, created during the Dada years. Richter was probably wrong when he situated Arp's discovery of torn paper in this period, since Arp himself places it a good ten years later, but again the randomness that it evoked was certainly present in the origins of the collages of colored squares and rectangles, as if their placement were the result of a chute, of a gust of wind, of a wrong move: "Like the disposition of planes, the proportion of these planes and their colors seemed to depend only upon chance, and I declared that these works were ordered 'according to the law of chance,' just like in the order of nature" (JE, p. 307). In the same spirit and always in favor of reducing personal intervention, Arp and Taeuber would no longer cut the paper they wished to attach themselves, but rather, would cut it with a guillotine. Vertical and horizontal compositions are obtained by placing side by side, without preconceived order, rectangles of different colors but of scrupulously equal size. Such a large work as *Geometrical Collage* from 1918 is a reticle of thirty equal rectangles, the proximity of two or three of those of the same color accentuating the "random" aspect of the composition. Arp was quickly to turn away from these investigations, which seemed to him to be rapidly exhausted, unlike the Dutch artists of *De Stijl*, who found in the right-angle placements an inexhaustible source.

Another discovery would turn out to be far richer for Arp: the relief. At the beginning, Arp's reliefs were done in wood; it took years for him to diversify the materials with which he worked. From the practice of collage and wood engraving, the intermediary form of the relief was born around 1917. One of the first, and without a doubt one of the most beautiful, *Forest* (1917), exists in two very similar versions. As was customary with Arp, the title is owed to the fact that one of the composition's pieces vaguely resembles the shape of a tree. But the whole is completely nonrepresentational: three layers of wood, irregularly cut, placed one on top of the other and held in place by a vise. Besides Arp's favorite colors, black and white, which are used discreetly here, the reds, yellows and greens attract the eye. And since the work is no longer derivative of a painting to be hung on the wall, but rather possesses a crucial thickness, the edges of the plaques of wood are painted as well: black, blue, white, red.... The work can be viewed at three quarters, or even in profile: it is already a polychrome sculpture, and it escapes completely the rectangle that traditionally delimits the painting, the collage and even certain reliefs. We should note that in other cases Arp, who had already incorporated the fluting of wood in his engravings, would not paint

Tzara, Richter and Arp, Zurich, 1918.

certain reliefs in order to leave unaltered the color and fiber of the edges of the wood.

The relief is a form so totally diverse in Arp's hands that he would continue to use it for the rest of his life, from the painted rectangle in which there are only one or two protuberant forms to the complex layers and — in a surprising way — to sculpture in three dimensions.

THROUGHOUT EUROPE

From 1918 onward, the Dadaists of Zurich were no longer isolated; they established contact with the most dynamic European and American avant-garde, and they knew that many of their ideas were shared by other young artists and writers. In 1917, Huelsenbeck returned to Berlin and took the good news about Dada with him; a Dada group was formed very quickly, with Grosz, Hausmann and the Herzfelde brothers, which was going to orient itself toward revolutionary agitation. Arp agreed to sign their 1918 manifesto. An alliance was thus formed with an artist who had nothing to envy in Dada, neither in spirit nor in creation: Francis Picabia. Picabia came to Switzerland toward the end of 1918. He was immediately received by the Zurich Dada group as one of their own, while he in turn opened the pages of his review *391* to them. Arp was to publish drawings, woodcuts and poems.

The end of 1918 finally brought peace. But that was not to mean the end of Dada in Zurich, for its events were to continue for still another year, especially in exhibitions in which Arp would participate. The collective event with the greatest repercussion, and the last one of such importance, took place on April 8, 1919. It was organized by Tzara, according to Richter, "with the precision and the splendor of a circus director." In preparation for the dance of the soirée, baptized *Noir Cacadou* (choreography by Taeuber), Arp and Richter built a backdrop: "On immense bands of paper two meters high, we began, Arp at one end and I at the other, to paint black abstractions. Arp's forms resembled huge cucumbers. I followed his example, and we ended up painting kilometers of cucumber beds, as I had nicknamed them, until we met in the middle. Then, we rolled all of it on pieces of wood in order to roll it up until it was time for the show." With respect to the dancers, it was Janco who had been chosen to make for them "the most excessive black masks," again in the words of Richter. Thus, the soirée was to consist of mayhem. The tension and ill humor of the public mounted as anti-melodic music by Schoenberg succeeded astounding poems cried out by several people at a time; and while Walter Serner read his aggressive manifesto *Letze Lockerung*, the public felt so insulted that gibes and jeers were no longer enough: a violent fistfight followed, all to the great satisfaction of the Dadaists. Such a coup could not be repeated, primarily because the public would be on guard and, moreover, because with the end of the war there were new places where it would be possible for Dada to take hold: Berlin, Paris and Cologne. The Zurich Dadaists would disperse in the last months of 1919. Arp went to Cologne and found his friend Max Ernst, who, with his friend Theodor Baargeld, had undertaken various subversive activities to shake off the torpor of a Rhineland occupied by the Allies.

In November, Arp exhibited with Ernst and Baargeld and collaborated on the only issue of *Bulletin D*; several months later, the no less ephemeral review *Die Schammade* would appear with some of his wood engravings. Arp and Ernst undertook a collaboration on a series of *Fatagaga* works, an unusual acronym for a no less unusual "Fabrication of Guaranteed Gasometrical Paintings." These are collages and montages done by Ernst and accompanied by equally disconcerting texts by Arp — seldom the other way around, it seems. The crowning achievement of Dada in Cologne was the First Dada Exhibition, which opened on April 20, 1920. Arp, Ernst and Baargeld presented work so provocative that the police temporarily closed the show. Arp was then invited to the International Dada Fair in Berlin, where the scandal was to be even greater. In Berlin not only did he meet the German Dadaists but also, in the significant Russian colony that had been established in the city, the Constructivist El Lissitzky, with whom he was to be linked in friendship.

But after Tzara rejoined Picabia in Paris, it was that city which became the most active center of Dada. In January 1920, thanks to the poets and painters convened by the group of the review *Littérature* (A. Breton, L. Aragon, Ph. Soupault), Dada was widely talked about; even while remaining in Germany, Arp could not be absent from it — Arp, wrote Breton in his *Entretiens*, "whose drawings and woodcuts are, without a doubt, at this

Tzara, Arp and Ernst, 1920.

moment, the most liberated and new which are available, and whose poems in German render the most original and moving sound." It was in this year that Arp published under the title *Der Vogel Selbdritt* and *Die Wolkenpumpe* the poems he had written in Zurich in the previous years. Here is a short poem from *Der Vogel Selbdritt*:

> the streams buck like rams in a tent.
> whips crack and from the hills come the crookedly combed shadows of the shepherds.
> black eggs and fools' bells fall from the trees.
> thunder drums and kettledrums beat upon the ears of the donkeys.
> wings brush against flowers.
> fountains spring up in the eyes of the wild boar.

> (*Gesammelte Gedichte I*, p. 41)
> (transl. Herbert Read)

Arp then published in the Parisian Dadaist review; he gladly illustrated their poems (Tzara, Péret); and he participated in their exhibitions, such as the Dada Salon in the Montaigne Gallery in 1921. He met Ernst, Tzara and Éluard in the Tyrol — in *Dada au grand air* he takes Tzara's part in the difference of opinion that pitted Éluard against Tzara — but on the whole, contrary to what happened in Zurich, Arp did not himself participate in the obtrusive and sometimes violent events of Parisian Dada. Scandal for scandal's sake, which is what was being practiced at that time, was not to his liking, nor was the judgmental aspect in which the Dadaists indulged in the trial of Barrès (1921), which had serious implications. Soupault had a beautiful way of explaining this slight difference in positions: "Arp was a discreet man who would surprise, but never create scandal" (*Vingt mille et un jours*).

Lissitzky, van Doesburg, Arp and Schwitters, 1922.

In addition, Arp had many other interests. In the years of restored peace between 1920 and 1925, he craved traveling: he circulated between Paris, Zurich, Rome and Hanover (1923, with Kurt Schwitters), and he collaborated in reviews that were generally more Constructivist than Dadaist (van Doesburg's and Mondrian's *De Stijl*, Vinea's and Janco's *Contimporanul*, Richter's *G*, Kassak's *Ma*, Schwitters' *Merz*, etc.). He was very much linked to Schwitters, who, fundamentally a Dadaist, nevertheless got along very well with the Constructivists. A significant event was the Constructivist Congress organized by the Bauhaus of Weimar in 1922: the old Zurich Dadaists (Arp, Tzara, Richter) not only met Schwitters again, but also van Doesburg, Lissitzky and Moholy-Nagy. From then on, Arp would be one of the few artists to find himself equally at ease in two tendencies that were in principle antithetical: Dada-Surrealism and Constructivism.

During these last convulsions of Dada, Arp continued to publish collections of poems, drawings and woodcuts. Otto Flake had published *8 Bois* in 1920 and Schwitters, under the title *7 Arpaden*, a group of seven lithographs in 1923. But Arp continued with his collages and reliefs. *Figure Bust* (1923) is cut and painted cardboard. It was also at this time, perhaps under the influence of Schwitters, that Arp began to use found objects: *Dada Kit* (1923) is a wooden board daubed and peeled and painted black, red or blue or even left as the artist found them. Arp would execute few works of this type and seemed to favor vividly colored creations in which blue dominated (the reliefs *Egg Iron* and *Shirtfront and Fork*, 1922, for example). He indulged in peculiar experiences in an attempt to integrate the frame into the work. *Infinitely Bound Form* (1923) is composed only of a small wood plaque fixed to a background of painted cardboard; its similarly painted frame is much larger than what is actually being framed.

SURREALISM

With Tzara out of the way and Dada definitely relegated to oblivion, the Parisian avant-garde finally reorganized itself around the *Littérature* group, and Breton finally brought out the *Surrealist Manifesto* in 1924. Arp immediately joined the Surrealists. In his eyes, it was a prolongation of Dada. In 1929 he was to clarify

this: "I did exhibitions with the Surrealists because their attitude revolted against 'art' and their attitude toward life itself was wise, as was Dada's" (JE, p. 406). More than theory, political commitment and collective manifestos — which it is true he would sign, but almost certainly due to friendship rather than conviction — it was poetry in all of its forms that linked Arp with Surrealism. He was not a gregarious man, and he scoffed at the café meetings that Breton imposed "on a troupe of poets, painters, very submissive, very obedient to their leader" (JE, p. 336). Arp was one of those who excused himself from those meetings: "Even at that time, I went infrequently to the literary cafés. The infantile vanity, the grotesque self-esteem of the habitués repelled me from the beginning. There was a great number of idiots who acted as if they could understand the incomprehensible.... I felt sorry to see men that I liked become more and more sterile" (Preface to *Wortträume und schwarze Sterne*). The real reasons for Arp's adherence to Surrealism are to be found in common methods of work, often inherited from Dada.

Poets like Breton, Soupault and Péret and painters like Miró, Ernst and Masson set great store by automatism. For Arp, it had already been a method of work. He had denounced in the Dada period what he called "the polishers." According to Arp, drawing, sculpture and poetry should originate in themselves; for him, this was a fundamental principle: "I allow myself to be guided by the work which is in the process of being born, I have confidence in it. I do not think about it. The forms arrive pleasant, or strange, hostile, inexplicable, mute, or drowsy. They are born from themselves. It seems to me as if all I do is move my hands" (JE, p. 435). He was in favor of the dream, the oneiricism so celebrated by the Surrealists: "Genesis, birth and eclosion often take place in a daydreaming state, and it is only later that the true sense of these considerations becomes apparent" (JE, p. 380). The process was always the same for Arp. Form comes first, then meaning. That is why he never knew *a priori* what the title of a work in progress was to be: "Each one of these bodies certainly signifies something, but it is only once there is nothing left for me to change that I begin to look for its meaning, that I give it a name" (JE, p. 383). If a work was entitled *Branches and Spectres Dancing*, or *Drawer Head*, or *Banner-Wheel*, it was not because the artist intentionally deformed existing objects, but rather that the forms born naturally from his hand *suggest such an association of ideas or the objects they resemble. If no association came to him, he would call it simply drawing, India ink, collage, or composition.*

Two white wooden forms painted with blue, in a frame similarly painted blue, is entitled *Lips and Handglass* (1927). A rounded double form, which comes to a cone at the top, is called *Pagoda Fruit* (1934). A small irregular dishlike form, which swells slightly, with another, more massive rounded form resting on it like a pensive, leaning head, is *Head and Shells* (1933). In some cases, it is impossible to discern the relationship between the forms and the names: Does *Dreaming* (1937) represent the shape of a dream, or a person dreaming? It is the spectator, in turn, who must dream. Why does *Sculpture To Lose In The Forest* (1932) designate three irregular elements filled in one over the other? It could be said that they are like the large stones sometimes found protruding from the soil in the forest, in Fontainebleau, in Coye-la-Forêt, or

Arp and Delaunay in Britanny, August 1929.

irrecognizably. The same organ can be deployed into a leaf of extreme complexity and then contract itself to form the simplest stalk. According to circumstances, the same organ can develop itself into a flowerbud or into a sterile twig. The calyx, perfecting itself, can develop a corolla; and the corolla can regress toward the calyx...." Even if we are not as convinced as Herbert Read of the influence on Arp of such observations, it is noticeable that plant metamorphosis and hybridization are more evident in Arp's career than in that of any other artist: from the late 'twenties, *Wings of the Forest* (painting, 1928), *Hand Fruit* (relief, 1928), *Leaves and Navels, Leaf Constellation, Head and Leaves* (reliefs, 1930), *Fruit of a Hand* (sculpture, 1930),... up until the last years, *Torso-Fruit, Initial of a Leaf, Bud on Goblet* (sculptures, 1960), *Page of a Floral Book* (relief-collage, 1960), *Floral Head* and *Pre-adamite Fruit* (sculptures, 1962. The titles of the works dedicated, in whole or in part, to the plant kingdom are infinitely more numerous than those dedicated to the animal world (from which Arp did not wish man to be distinguished). Contrary to Goethe, Arp did not seek to justify himself; his position is not an intellectual one. André Breton was correct in relating it to that of a child in one of the most beautiful pages dedicated to Arp, in his *Anthologie de l'humour noir,* of which at least this essential remark will be remembered: "As we liked to do as children, extracting from the soft forest floor the light chestnut trees only a few centimeters high at the base of which the chestnut continues to shine to the sun its clods of soil from the past, the chestnut conserving all of its presence and witnessing with its presence the power of green hands, of shadow, of airy white or pink pyramids, of dances... and of future chestnuts which, under new dust, would be discovered by the marvelled sight of other children. It is in this perspective that the work of Arp, more than any other, should be situated. He found the most vital in himself in the secrets of this germinating life where the most minimal detail is of the greatest importance, where, on the other hand, the distinction between the elements becomes meaningless, adopting a peculiar *under the rock* humor permanently." Among the Surrealists, such homages are not unusual, and it is surprising that it has sometimes been suggested that the Surrealists did not appreciate the importance of Arp among their ranks.

anywhere; it is as if they were eroded by the sea that deposited them there, one over the other, as in a painting by Yves Tanguy, or they could be stones for Tom Thumb; it would be enough to take this sculpture and lose it in the forest to give it back to its original destiny: a good sculpture, according to Arp, participates in nature and is one of its elements. The Surrealists themselves were surprised by this good-natured magic, by this faculty of playful imagination: "Like in many Surrealist works, Arp's paintings are done with magic. But with a particular kind of magic, the magic of heartfelt joy. How to explain the euphoria which penetrates us in this universe of eternal spring, this plenitude of the senses, this thirst for the heavens." Or: "He systematically makes forms buckle, making everything similar to everything else, sets illusory classifications and the very hierarchy of things held to be true on end. He amuses himself with the world like an imp escaped from the forest acts in social relations in the magnificent manner of a dog in a game of ninepins." Thus Robert Desnos and Michel Leiris, respectively, expressed themselves the day after the exhibition presented in the Surrealist gallery of Camille Goemans. In fact, this magical mentality that so surprised them situates Arp in the line of German Romanticism and of the poets whom he imitated in his youth. He obtained pleasure in reading the ballads and popular songs collected by Arnim and Brentano in *Des Knaben Wunderhorn* (1806). Like his distant ancestors, Arp was willing to welcome metamorphosis, sculpture, like nature, being for him a field of perpetual transformations. Herbert Read has correctly related Arp to a passage by Goethe in which he attributed to himself a scientific beginning. "The organic parts of a plant — leaves and flowers, stamens and pistils, the great variety of plant tissues and everything which affect the senses — are all identical organs which a series of botanical operations modify and transform

A SURREALIST SCULPTOR

It was a Surrealist, the Aragon of *La peinture au défi* (1930), who was the first to show how the relief questioned art, in that it rejected at the same time the myth of the inspired artist, an exceptional being, and the sacrosanct métier: "Arp had his reliefs executed by the joiner; it was a concession if he colored them himself, and when they became dirty, they could be repainted without annoying their author. His pictorial standards are new, and it is pure idiocy to be surprised by them." The relief, by the use that is made of the work of a third party, is very similar to a collage in that it is difficult to conserve. Perishable, the relief attempts to achieve the noble and the intemporal — through marble, bronze and oil — to such an extent that one can repaint it oneself. It is probably also in this spirit, in order to show that the unique character of a work does not add anything to its beauty, that Arp would later make "multiples" of certain of his works, as in *Star, Bird Mask* (1966) and other découpages in golden watchmaking metals.

Although Arp belonged to the Surrealist group, he maintained principles of independence more characteristic of Dada. Thus, he did not refrain from participating in other events that had nothing to do with Surrealism. In the same year in which he participated in the First Surrealist Exhibition in Paris (1925), he published the book *Les Ismes de l'art*, of Constructivist tendencies, with El Lissitzky. The following year, with Taeuber and van Doesburg, he undertook vast abstract compositions to decorate the halls of the Aubette, a café-restaurant-dance hall-movie theater in the center of Strasbourg. This work was to take them two years; little appreciated by the local public, the building would be destroyed ten years later. It was during this period that Arp installed himself in a house-studio in Meudon built according to Taeuber's plans.

The larger task of the Aubette did not prevent Arp from continuing his personal work: string reliefs or polychrome reliefs like *Lips and Handglass* (1927) and numerous graphic works — in India ink like the simple blot entitled *Flower*, or in gouache like the two or three eyes of color, on a black or white background, from 1928. Representation seems to make a discreet return in drawings like *The Priests of Florence* (1927), in which, among vague comical silhouettes, a hand or a face can be distinguished. It is especially in the Surrealist period that Arp allowed deliberately realistic details to appear in his graphic works, with a farcical intention; thus a sort of lichen taking the form of a double hand or foot, hence the title *Hand Foot* (1932), is composed of three conspicuous finger- or toenails.

It was between 1928 and 1930 that Arp was to begin really sculpting — that is to say, creating sculpture in the round, designed to be placed in a spatial setting and not hung on a wall. He had practiced sculpture in the round at different times in his youth. After 1915, unhappy with the results, he destroyed all such sculpture. Actually, he had been working for some time with cut and painted wooden boards, which, instead of being attached flatly to one another, were placed at right angles so that one served as a base for the next, creating a sort of "posed relief." It is also possible that certain wood sculptures mechanically cut with a saw and modeled in the round facilitated the progress from relief to sculpture in the round. *One Large and Two Small* (1931) consists of a large flat form in the shape of a keyhole and two small amphora shapes, perfectly rounded and with vertical symmetry, all three elements posed on a circular wood plaque. But Arp did not need intermediary stages — first of all because he had already practiced modeling, and second because there is photographic proof that he had already modeled sculptures beforehand (notably, in 1929 the review *Variétés* had published two reproductions). In 1930, he created the celebrated *Head of an Imp* called "Kaspar" in allusion to the poem "Hélas notre bon Kaspar est mort" which Arp had published ten years earlier — a sort of a bust with three mischievous points evoking the nose, the chin and the pointed cap of a gnome. But generally — whether they were modeled in plaster and then cast in bronze or cement

The surrealists in 1930: Tzara, Éluard, Breton, Arp, Dalí, Tanguy, Ernst, Crevel and Man Ray.

or, less frequently, directly carved in stone — Arp was fond of rounded forms, whether of a single piece like his diverse *Human Concretions* (1934-35) or *Moonfruit* (1936), adorned with openwork like *Crown of Buds* (1936) or of two or more forms placed side by side like *Head and Shell* (1933), *Pagoda Fruit* (1934) or *Constellation* (1938), in which four shell shapes emerge from a large wheel. The problem of representation was not posed any more often in Arp's sculpture than in any of the other media in which he worked; the naming occurred after the sculpture was finished, according to what it suggested to the imagination. Even though his work was nonrepresentational, Arp disapproved of the term "abstract art" being applied to it, as he often explained: "We do not wish to copy nature. We do not want to reproduce, we want to produce. We want to produce as a plant produces a fruit and does not itself reproduce. We want to produce directly and without mediation. As there is not the least trace of abstraction in this art, we will call it concrete art" (JE, p. 183).

Arp sometimes felt the need to break with rounded forms, either by opposing two types of sculpture or by breaking the forms of a single mass. *Human Concretion on Goblet* (1935-37) places in opposition one of these natural forms in which the work of the human hand can be seen, as Arp described it, and a neat and impeccably flat, cutout goblet base, added in 1947. The roundness of the concretion is contrasted with the rectitude of the goblet, with which it comes into contact at two or three points, depending on the way in which one chooses to place them. Or, in *Milestone* (1938), two cylinders forming an obtuse angle bury themselves in a rounded mass that opens into a lip-like shape, accentuating the perception of precarious balance; this sculpture in wood, created in collaboration with Taeuber, and the difference in the two artists' temperaments as well as in their esthetics explain the contrasting form. Another sculpture in wood conceived in collaboration with Taeuber is *Conjugal Sculpture* (1937), in which a sole structure bulges twice, presenting several distinct sections of roundness, while the whole rests on a perfect cylinder that is crushed by its mass. Even more than in *Milestone*, the rectitude of the sections emphasizes the grooves and grain of the wood.

In wood, in plaster, in hard stone or in metal, rectangular or curved, the sculptures, like the reliefs, are always marked by an exemplary polish and sharpness. This type of sculpture has sometimes been related to Neolithic art (Carl Einstein called it "Neolithic infancy" in 1929). For fun, and doubtlessly out of admiration for it, Arp himself had alluded to Cycladic art. *Seated* (1937) is in fact subtitled *In Remembrance of the Cyclades*; but only the polish of the sculpture recalls their art (in which reclining figures are infrequent) in this semi-reclining form; it also recalls the Lion of Belfort. The relationship that might exist between Arp and his great predecessor Constantin Brancusi is also a question that needs to be posed. In about 1920, Arp went to visit Brancusi in his home, and thirty-five years later he gave an ambiguous account of this visit. He acknowledges that "*Mademoiselle Pogany* is the fairy godmother of abstract sculpture," but adds: "It was my first and last visit to Brancusi. Is this insinuation to be understood? I won't explain any more because I never went back to visit him again, and today I would never express anything except my deep admiration for Brancusi" (JE, p. 422). It is possible that, just as Brancusi fled very quickly from Rodin because, he said, seedlings could not grow underneath large trees, Arp feared the weight of his elder. But, taking into account that Arp had spoken of "abstract sculpture" with respect to Brancusi, it is evident that he did not include him in his own realm of *concrete art*. Their processes of thought were antithetical: while Arp worked on forms of which the subject did not originate in reality, Brancusi always began with a subject — the head of a woman or a seal — and abstracted from it a purer and purer form. Arp understood that from his first visit and knew that there was nothing he could learn from such a method — an admirable one, to be sure, but one not useful in his search for the principles of *natural* creation.

There does exist an *Automatic Sculpture* called *Homage to Rodin,* from 1938. It is a work brutally and rapidly shaped, then left in accordance with the automatic working principles, which do not admit correction (the method Breton and Soupault used in *Magnetic Fields*). The raw, massive work, without real polish, is exceptional in Arp's sculpture (nevertheless, two works done at Trèves should be mentioned). We should wonder whether that is not another ironic homage to a great precursor; however, while Arp never denied the admiration he had felt for Rodin in his youth, he tended to distance himself afterwards.

THE ABSTRACTION-CREATION PERIOD

Shortly after settling in Paris, Arp and Taeuber became friendly with Michel Seuphor. When he created the *Documents Internationaux de l'Esprit Nouveau,* Seuphor invited Arp to participate. Only one issue of the review was published. A bit longer-lived, the Franco-Polish magazine *L'art contemporain,* by Seuphor's close friend Jan Brzekowski, was published in three issues between 1929 and 1930, on which Arp willingly collaborated. Finally, in 1930, Seuphor had the idea of organizing a regrouping of artists; assisted by the painter Joaquin Torres-Garcia, he founded Cercle et Carré. As its name suggests, this association was reserved for abstract artists with geometrical tendencies, the opposite of Surrealism in some ways. International stars like Kandinsky and Mondrian joined, as well as creators as little known as Marcelle Cahn or the Mexican Germán Cueto. In 1930,

three issues of the magazine with the same title appeared and an exposition took place which had certain repercussions. Arp was certainly present there, as it allowed him to express his opposition to a new tendency that had appeared in Surrealism, mainly represented by Salvador Dalí and René Magritte: "In recent times, Surrealist painters have used descriptive illusionistic academic methods" (JE, p. 63), he wrote to Brzekowski at the time. Cercle et Carré having disappeared too rapidly, the abstract artists felt the need to regroup again, both against Surrealism and against a certain return to representation in painting throughout Europe toward the end of the 'twenties. Thus Abstraction-Creation was born.

It was at the initiative of Auguste Herbin that Abstraction-Creation was founded in 1931. Georges Vantongerloo was the director and Jean Hélion the secretary. Herbin had been one of Arp's first friends upon his arrival in Paris; it was thus foreseeable that Arp was to be one of the founding members of the new association. Very quickly, a good part of the group from Cercle et Carré was to meet again in a very large organization, rubbing elbows with old Cubists like Léger, Villon, Gleizes, the Delaunays and numerous foreigners such as Baumeister, Pevsner and Wadsworth. The most diverse artists, as long as they were not Figurative or Surrealist, were allowed to join Abstraction-Creation, whose activities (collective expositions, debates, publication of a magazine) were to take place between 1931 and 1934. Although always linked to the Surrealists, Arp was not to feel uncomfortable in the heart of Abstraction-Creation until 1934, when it became too dogmatic in favor of Geometrical Abstraction. Always faithful to his principle of liberty ("Those who join us retain their freedoms," said the *Dada Manifesto 1918*), Arp was then to abandon the group with Taeuber.

Arp and Sophie Taeuber, Laval, 1939.

It was characteristic of Arp not to bind himself to any constraints except those he chose freely. Independent without being an obstinate individualist, Arp liked collaborating with others. Besides Taeuber, with whom he would frequently collaborate, he was to work from time to time with van Rees, Richter, Ernst, van Doesburg and many others. These communal experiences were one of the things he appreciated about the Surrealists. He willingly drew "exquisite cadavers" with them. In 1931, he wrote *Trois nouvelles exemplaires* in collaboration with Vicente Huidobro. He would repeat this experience in 1938-39 when he participated in the novel *L'homme qui a perdu son squelette* with Leonora Carrington, Marcel Duchamp, Paul Éluard, Max Ernst and several other friends.

Arp certainly had preferences; he was not afraid to voice opinions, but he mistrusted dogmatism and detested intolerance. That explains why he felt closer to someone like Kandinsky than to someone like Mondrian, who could not stand the sight of a tree. Arp loved nature and wanted to filter himself into it without copying it, which fundamentally differentiates him from Mondrian. This was the cause of a perpetual difference of opinion between them about which Arp had commented: "It was only in our time that painting and sculpture were liberated from aspects of a mandolin, from a president in tails, from battle, from landscape. I like nature, but not its substitutes. Naturalist art, illusionism, is a substitute for nature. I remember that in arguing with Mondrian, he opposed art to nature saying that art is artificial and nature is natural. I do not share his opinion. I do not think that nature is in natural opposition to art. Art's origins are natural" (JE, p. 317). It was a conviction that was never to change. A haughty attitude seemed out of place to him: "Anyone who would become wild with joy for having drawn a square would put us in good spirits" (JE, p. 359), he said, when he and Taeuber would discover that at the same time they themselves were painting squares, other artists (Mondrian, Malevitch) were not only doing likewise, but also extracting rigid theories from them. For Arp, neither the artist nor his art are outside of nature; and the corollary of this was a modest attitude of which anyone who has known Arp is a witness.

Arp was never a partisan of art without risk of unforeseen events; it seemed to him that Dalí, as well as Mondrian, worked in that way. It is not by chance, then, that he introduced into his work in the early thirties a new technique very much in the spirit of the spontaneity and randomness so cherished by Dada: torn paper. In itself, it is a very simple thing: one or several leaves of paper are torn, and the pieces are glued to paper or cardboard. No one had yet thought of it at the time of the exposition of collages "Painting Defied" at Goemans in 1930. It is not a simple evolution of Cubist *papier collé* or Surrealist collage, but a new esthetic development. Arp related it to his first longings for perfection in the use of paper — paper having preoccupied him much more than canvas and oil painting: "Ever since my childhood, I was haunted by the search for perfection. An imperfectly cut paper literally made me ill, I would guillotine it. My collages came undone, they became blistered. I then introduced death and decay in my compositions. I reacted by avoiding any precision from one day to another. Instead of cutting the paper, I would tear it with my hands" (JE, p. 431). The imprecision of this gesture anticipates the inevitable process of destruction of all works — particularly of collages, works more fragile than others. Chance remains the same, and Arp himself tore the paper; while other artists like him, with origins in Dada, remitted themselves to chance not dependent upon themselves: Schwitters collected scrap objects, and Duchamp let intemperate weather alter the pages of a treatise on geometry that he hung outside a window.

Arp dates his first torn papers toward 1932. They are fragments of black paper dispersed over a white background. This contrast of black and white recalls some of the India ink drawings, particularly those of 1916-18, but the cutting of the pieces of paper, their ragged edges formed by the fibers, gives the work a certain depth not present in the inkblots or in the collages of paper cut by scissors or by the guillotine. This was to characterize all of the work in torn paper, even after Arp made the technique more complicated. Instead of tearing paper of the same color, he would tear sheets of different colors and assemble the pieces. He would eventually complete the torn fragments with crayon, ink or gouache. In effect, they were drawings that he would tear in order to reassemble the fragments. Such a *Torn Drawing* from 1938 was composed from a previously existing drawing in India ink. Arp would even come to use old wood engravings that he had done fifteen or twenty years earlier as bases for his torn-paper works. It was a matter of destroying a work to give it another life, another chance. During the 'thirties, Arp had not yet begun to use works by others to make his "torn papers," but it was easy to guess that it eventually would occur.

The differences in the torn papers were not only in their colors or in what they represented, but also in their very texture: certain papers produce jagged edges when they are torn; others, composed of layers of different colors or fibers, show tears that contrast with their surface. Arp knew how to profit from all of these characteristics. The virtual absence of newspaper or printed paper from the great variety of papers he used is notable. That is because Arp's torn papers are fundamentally different from Cubist *papiers collés*. Braque, Picasso and Gris deliberately used printed paper, less for the trompe l'œil effect than for its texture, the design of its letters and, above all, for the verbal puns that could be achieved by a certain word, by one expression or another. Arp, on the contrary, did not want to add exterior intellectual meanings to the forms. Nor do his collages have anything to do with those of Max Ernst. As always, in all of Arp's work, forms were born without preconceived ideas. If one form or another suggested the representation of a particular idea, it would remain subjective, variable and, in any case, *a product of chance*, with all the malicious insistence with which Arp was capable of investing these terms.

The torn papers were such unusual works that Arp waited some time before revealing them to the public. Too abstract for Surrealism, they were too casually Dada for Abstract circles like Abstraction-Creation. This delay was also due to modesty and negligence, all the more as from 1937 Arp would have a convenient platform, the magazine *Plastique*.

It was in 1937 that Sophie Taeuber, with the help of Arp and César Domela, published the first issue of

Plastique. Financed by two American Maecenases, due to the war the magazine unfortunately would not be published in more than five issues. It manifested the double link of Arp to Surrealism on the one hand and to nonrepresentative art on the other. At the beginning, the magazine was above all Constructivist; Domela, a renegade from the *De Stijl* group, would publish one of the first articles about Malevitch in French. A special issue would be dedicated to the Abstract Americans. But little by little, Surrealism would take up almost all the space in the magazine (notably, with *L'homme qui a perdu son squelette*, the novel written collectively by the Surrealists), which would cause Domela's retreat. Arp, Duchamp, Éluard and Ernst would no longer have the chance to work together, since the war would disperse them.

During the 'thirties, the Arps would see tension rise in several European countries. After 1933, refugees began to flow from Germany to France, among them artist and writer friends of theirs. They forced themselves to continue their respective work in spite of it all. We have previously mentioned graphic works done in common and sculptures like *Milestone* and *Conjugal Sculpture*. It was perhaps through Taeuber's influence that Arp returned to oil painting; an example of his work in this period, *Duo Painting* (1939), displays the conjunction of geometrical lines and two small circles over light. There is nothing tragic here, not any more so than in any other works by Arp. That is because his art is not destined to express the tragic, to trouble or to worry, but to reassure, to cause joy or to encourage peaceful meditation. However, there is perhaps a certain state of tension, signs of disquiet, in certain *papiers déchirés.*

THE WAR

Fearing serious problems with the Nazis, the Arps left their house in Meudon in June 1940, just before the occupation of Paris. They would wander throughout the

Sophie Taeuber, Susie Magnelli, Arp and Sonia Delaunay, Grasse, 1942.

summer — first in Dordogne, where they met Domela and Gabrielle Buffet, then in Annecy at Peggy Guggenheim's. At the end of September, they settled at Grasse near Alberto and Susi Magnelli. They spent more than two years there together; their small group of friends would widen when Sonia Delaunay joined them after the death of Robert Delaunay. In spite of the war, of the worries about the future and of the always disappointing attempt to obtain a visa for America, which was never to materialize, this was to be an extremely fruitful period: "In the dark, unreal years of 1941 and 1942, the reality of beauty was the only consolation of our little circle in Grasse" (JE, p. 277).

The period was characterized by a number of important works involving the direct cutting of stone; in spite of the war, Arp was able to obtain marble from a local dealer (after the war, he would from time to time cast these works in bronze). Some of them are along the lines of his work in the thirties. *The Leaf* (1941), for example, is an elongated, rounded form, static, like a fallen leaf. Others mark the appearance of new forms. *Clawed alouette* (1942) is disquieting not only because of its title, evoking the cruelty of wolves and the claws that hold sway over the period, but also by its structure, which is that of a hydra whose claw seems to clutch the base. *Mediterranean Sculpture* (1941-42), of which two versions exist, is an oblong and polished form, a flattened oval marking a return to symmetry; erected on a parallelepiped base, it is more than a reference to Brancusi; its elementary form has the authority of a primitive idol like those of the Mediterranean sculptures of the ancient Cyclades.

Arp was also innovative in his reliefs, some of which were in marble, others in wood. Among the latter is *Triptych* (1942). The assembly of three reliefs of the same size, in which calm oval forms float, is rendered more dynamic by the fact that one is blue and the other two are white and that, contrary to all expectations, the blue relief would not be in the center but rather on one of the sides: conspicuous asymmetry that almost propels the triptych, as if it were moving itself along the wall.

But more than ever, paper seems to be the favorite material of the artist. With India ink, he composes fantasy patterns in black, forms very different from those of the Dada days, which are less likely to tease a smile. Some are no longer on white backgrounds, but rather on beige. In others, Arp wanted to accentuate the uncertainty of the technique by drawing directly in India ink with his finger; the strokes are large and irregular, and the uniformity of the black that characterizes the ink is no longer the desired effect; on the contrary, the deliberate inequality of color, the stuttering effect and the smearing all go beyond spontaneity, beyond Dadaist chance and Surrealist automatism to attain a brute and Cobra art. In fact, the artists of Cobra have great respect for the graphic works of Arp, who is certainly, in the case of these works, one of their most obvious precursors.

Arp also did collages and *papier déchiré*, within an entire range of techniques: a simple black-and-white effect with a glued form (*Collage*, 1941), an aquarelle *papier déchiré* (*Composition 1*, 1942) or an India-ink design torn and glued to a cream background (*Torn Drawing*, 1942). One of these works is a *Collage* (1941-42) that belonged to Mrs. Magnelli. In this case, several photographs of *Human Concretion* were torn and then glued; a green gouache was then applied to the whole, and since the color was applied almost evenly, the concretions seem to float in a greenish-blue haze. The work is an example of one of the most beautiful Surrealist effects.

It was in Grasse that the first *papiers froissés* appeared. After having torn the paper, Arp would crumple it — the very negation of centuries of protecting drawings from the dangers of wrinkling or tearing! It is therefore an enrichment for the artist, who, as opposed to other artists who advance in "periods" and abandon a theme or method after having exhausted it, continued from then on to exploit all the discoveries he possibly could make at the same time. It could be said that he did not proceed by advancing but by constantly widening his repertoire of methods. Like Arp's other methods of expression, the crumpling of paper was also to undergo a development. The paper was sometimes wrinkled after having been painted or covered by a drawing; other times, the process was reversed. The second solution seems to have been the more frequent, because the unequal qualities of the paper's surface caused an unpredictable distribution of the paint when Arp would trace his forms or blots. *Crumpled Paper* of 1942 is just an abstract drawing with large black strokes, but since oil paint had been used in addition to gouache on the crumpled wrapping paper that serves as a support, in the light the work acquires a mobility from one facet to another that could never have been achieved in a work painted with orthodox methods on one kind of paper. More, perhaps, than the reliefs, the crumpled papers are related to sculpture because of the tactile aspects of their fabrication while the artist crumples the paper in his hands, while he flattens it out and while he studies the uneven parts of which he is going to take advantage in his work.

With Magnelli, Sonia Delaunay and, of course, Taeuber, Arp did a series of lithographs that can be discussed here even though they were not printed until after the war, in 1950. Gabrielle Buffet assumed, probably correctly, that Arp was the originator of this project: "Who, among this group of friends, all of them familiar with and expert technicians of abstract art, would have had the idea of starting a creation game among them? Arp, without a doubt, always haunted by the example of the cathedral builders. One of the four would inscribe the first motif, which would then be developed by the three others, each one working, in turn, on the same piece of paper." The experience was similar, then, to the "exquisite cadavers" of the Surrealists, but Arp himself has remarked that the spirit was different because of the historical circumstances: "1941. We met in Grasse. The stars which had reunited these four artists were especially favorable to work in collaboration, because the tragic hours during which these lithographs were conceived obliged them to modesty, to the sacrifice of all vanity, to the effacement of too individual expressions" (JE, p. 340). A work in common, rather than a search for originality.

All of this work did not prevent worry from assailing the fugitives in Grasse, whose daily lives were precarious even in the unoccupied zone: there was rationing, and the return to Paris was forbidden. Contrary to his friend Max Ernst, who, as a German citizen, was committed to a period in a French camp before managing to flee to America, Arp became French. At the beginning of the war, he translated his first name from Hans to Jean. But, to the extent to which the situation deteriorated in France,

he did not feel safe from being bothered and even feared persecution. In the collection of poems symptomatically entitled *Poèmes sans prénoms*, which he published in 1941 at his own expense, distress is much more evident than in his plastic works:

Blocks of dawn collapse
accompanied by the famished cooing
of the mystery turtledove...

(JE, p. 167).
(transl. S. Fauchereau)

In anger, Arp even composed a short story in which, contrary to the rest of his work, an explicit meaning appeared. Under scarcely symbolic appearances, the maniac who is the hero is no less recognizable than the caricatures that George Grosz or Otto Dix, old cronies from Dada, would make of him: "With a diabolical élan, with the joyous cry of a Tyrolean defenestrator who dances around a lake of grease, he rushed to the accumulated objects and threw them through the majestic window of the great works. It was his life to throw all that existed from the window" (JE, p. 179). This text, *Le grand sadique à tout casser*, was published in 1942 by the Surrealist group, "The Hand with a Pen", with a caricature by Maurice Henry. But one did not mock the "great sadist" with impunity at the time he was at the height of his powers. It was necessary to flee like Ernst or Grosz, or to be persecuted like Dix, or even to be massacred like Otto Freundlich, Max Jacob and Robert Desnos, old friends of Arp.

Arp and Taeuber decided to cross the border to Switzerland on November 14, 1943. Welcomed by Max Bill, Arp began to work again (*The Sand Sphere*, 1943, black torn paper on white from a pre-war drawing). For Max Bill, who was to publish it in 1945, he collected a selection of woodcuts; in these, *Eleven Configurations*, the grain of the wood appears in the black of the ink, giving the forms a particularly sensual quality. All this activity in the pleasure of newfound security was about to be brutally interrupted. On January 13, 1943, Sophie Taeuber died in Zurich, asphyxiated by the fumes from a coal stove. It was an accident according to most, and if there were a few voices claiming suicide, it did not change the fact that the twentieth century had just lost an important artist. Arp collapsed, and his work was terribly affected by the loss. He himself was well aware of it in the numerous texts and poems that he would not cease to dedicate to Taeuber from them on, the first of them written the day after her death:

You took leave clearly and calmly.
With you life was sweet.
Your last canvas was completed.
Your brushes were neatly put away.

(JE, p. 188)
(transl. Herbert Read)

This death would have grave consequences for Arp. Gabrielle Buffet, an old friend, explains the artist's attitude: "The living source of his being was affected by this brutal blow, it would take him years to recover his balance. An acute mystical crisis would drive him to enter a religious order for a time. The affectionate insistence of his friends was essential for him to decide to undertake creative activity again. He wrote poems with a seriousness of which we had not suspected him. A series of aquarelles from 1944 marked an attempt at a new technique. It was only in 1947 that he would really return to sculpture per se." Between 1942 and 1947 he did no new sculptures, scarcely a half dozen wood reliefs and an extremely reduced amount of graphic work. The end of the war was a gray and sterile period for the artist.

When he left the cloister that he had entered after Sophie Taeuber's death, Arp took up some of his old activities, especially wash drawing. Then some friends convinced him to participate in some collective expositions; he would accept, but with the condition that Taeuber's work be presented along with his, a principle to which he would hold from then on in almost all of his personal exhibits. He gathered Taeuber's work together, making sure that it was known. Even though he had a new companion, Marguerite Hagenbach, a longtime friend, Taeuber was the inspiration for much of Arp's literary and plastic work of the 'forties.

RETURN TO PARIS

After World War II, with its rationing and the fear of nuclear war, the world began to recover in the midst of its ruins, and Arp was in an uncharacteristically pessimistic phase: "In the frightful chaos of our time, only a few oases of purity still appear to me. Man has succumbed to the frenzy of intelligence; this demential being impregnated with scientific culture tries to dominate the world with his pseudo-head. His inhumanity leads him into a sordid labyrinth from which he will find no escape. Money and the machine are the idols he fervently adores, his joy in progress knows no limits — he measures — he calculates — he weighs — he makes fire — he pulverizes — he kills — he cuts across the sky — he burns — he lies — he boasts — he drops bombs, and that is the way he distinguishes himself from the beasts. Through his infernal intelligence, he surpasses everything that lives. In his folly he creates in the infinite, as well as the confusion of his spirit and his love for order" (JE, p. 215). It is important to take these words at their face value in order to understand why Arp produced so little in these years.

Arp had meanwhile found a means of continuing his collaboration with Taeuber. Tearing a drawing, an engraving, or reproductions, he could rearrange the pieces into a new work; *Collage* (1946) was obtained in this way, and, just as in the past, it was a *duo*. "Was I dreaming when I saw Sophie, luminous and calm, against a background of clear white petals, in a clear, white star? Was I dreaming when I heard Sophie speaking in me, and that we spent a while like that? Was I dreaming when I saw Sophie, living, serenely dead and having died serenely, chiseled thus in a gem which I have in my real hands?" (JE, p. 280). Arp was to do a number of *duos* in this way over the course of the years to come. He would even apply the same process to other artists as well.

In 1946, Arp went back to Meudon. He settled there without abandoning Basel, where Marguerite Hagenbach lived, as a second residence. He undertook an artistic life

again, participating in diverse expositions. Arp collected all of his poems in French and published them in *Siège de l'air* (1946). Above all, he had the satisfaction of finding in the Denise René Gallery a place to exhibit as he liked, where his work would from then on be defended. In 1947, the year of the International Surrealist Exposition organized by Breton in Paris and in which he naturally collaborated, Arp was back to full activity.

Not content with enlarging his field of activity in all of the years that were to follow, Arp took up some of his previous works and began to revise them. We have already mentioned that the *Human Concretion* of the 'thirties had been placed on a *Goblet*. The sculpture thus resulted in an antithetical form, *Human Concretion on Goblet* (1948). Flowing forms appeared, like *Bird Skeleton* (1947), a sharp, fragile structure, rising into the air; or, on the contrary, massive forms: *Mythical Sculpture* (1949) is a rounded idol, like a Buddha with arms and legs crossed; or stacked-up structures, about whose origins Marguerite Hagenbach has spoken with respect to *Three Super-imposed Goblets* (1947): "For Arp, even in his child-hood, the base which permits a sculpture to stand up was on the one hand a motive for gaiety, inciting him to mischief, on the other, a motive for preoccupation. That is why he has created so many sculptures which do not need bases. Their position might be lying on the grass, or crouching on a piece of furniture, or in the niche of a wall. For other sculptures he created forms on which they were posed and he called them *goblets*. This sculpture is an autonomous creation composed of several goblets." If many of Arp's sculptures give a reassuring impression of stability, these appear to be in a precarious equilibrium: one gets the urge to seize them, to slide one over the other. We find this type of sculpture in *Nameless Figure* (1957), in which three hewn blocks are stacked one upon the other as if one had sawed apart and then reassembled a sculpture. The affect would be diversified later by placing two or three goblets stacked diagonally beneath the sculptures (the *Daphne*, for example).

In his sculptures, Arp sometimes used direct hewing. He executed a series of works in chalky stone in 1950, *Ghostly Cavernous Lunar Landscape, Pistil, Frond...*,

F. Richter, Kiessler, X, Arp, X, Marguerite Hagenbach, Richter, 1949.

which he then often cast in bronze or in other materials in order to give them several lives. In addition to this process of frequent reproduction, Arp sometimes enlarged the works. The most celebrated of his works carried out in this way has quite a story behind it. *Impish Form* was born in 1949, about forty centimeters high, in plaster, in marble and in bronze. But four years later, Arp decided to change the format due to a sudden inspiration that he had described: "At daybreak I found on my sculptor's turntable a little mischievous form, alert and somewhat obese, with a stomach like a lute. It seemed to me like an imp. I called it that. And all of a sudden one day this little character, this imp, through a Venezuelan medium, found itself to be the father of a giant. This giant son resembles its father like an egg resembles another egg, a fig another fig, a bell another bell'' (JE, p. 396). Animal, vegetable or fashioned by the human hand, everything in this process is natural to Arp. Ten times as large, the imp tripod of 1949 became the *Cloud Shepherd* of 1953 in the University City of Caracas, a bronze more than three meters high. This adventure was not to be so unusual in the sculpted work of Arp and would happen with *Three Superimposed Goblets* (1947), *Howl* (1957), *Small Meudon Venus* (1956), *Torso of a Muse* (1959) and *Torso-Fruit* (1960), among other works. We note that, as with *Cloud Shepherd,* considerable enlargements were often made with the intention of obtaining a monumental sculpture for a public place. *Threshold Object*, which was only seventy centimeters high at its birth in 1965, has tripled in height to adorn a square in its native town.

Arp sometimes proceeded by amplifying the forms of a single work. The best example of this is the *Ptolemy* series, curly figures, hollow and divided (like the mushrooms called "clathres"). *Ptolemy I* (1958) is one meter high, and two interior branches divide its space into three caverns. *Ptolemy II* (1958) is also one meter high, but the body is complicated, with three branches forming five openings. Finally, *Ptolemy III* (1961) is more than two meters high. It tends toward a symmetry that makes it more majestic; its branches are not as numerous, and they seem to divide the interior space into more harmonious cavities.

For his sculptures, as for the rest of his work, Arp borrows forms from the whole of the natural world, which, for the purpose of his titles, gives the impression of covering a number of themes much larger than that of any other artist before him. There are the plants: *Pistil* (1950), *Between Leaf and Bird* (1959), *Initial of a Leaf* (1960); the animals: *Bird Skeleton* (1947), *Howl* (1951), *Configuration with Snake Movements* (1955), *Animal Conscious of its Beauty* (1957); man: *Evocation of a Human Form* (1950), *Great Personality* (1957), *Drawer Head* (1960); the inanimate elements: *Frond* (1950), *Meudon Knot* (1957), *Spiny-Handled Heart* (1958), *Star* (1960); and, finally, the sentiments: *Anguishing Configuration* (1955) and *Sinuous Simplicity* (1960).

Of course, sculpture was not Arp's only activity. During all of these years, he was creating in all domains. Among the reliefs, *Echo Mirror* (1958) should be mentioned. It is based on large red strokes in oil paint over a yellow background. The fifties were rich in gouaches, such as *Wings of the Forest* (1955), where perpendicular and round forms unbalance the rectangle of the frame, or *Constellation of Five Forms* (1956), of blue dark as the night sky in which float yellow and white blots; but *Branches of Spectres Dancing* is a wash drawing. Collages and torn papers are equally numerous. Some of the collages have unusual formats, such as the *Collage* from 1956, which is very high, with the black and beige elements one above the other. It sometimes happened that Arp cut an engraving and recomposed it, but it was more likely that he would tear. If that were to be the case, the materials were apt to be diverse: *Torn Paper* from 1954 is one of his own woodcuts, torn and glued to cardboard; the *Collage* from 1950-53 is an assembly on a cream background of fragments of a photograph of a rug by Taeuber. Arp also created a whole series with a friend. With Michel Seuphor in 1956, he entered into a veritable collaboration. *Lightning Flash* tears lines and ribbons from the original work to reassemble them according to a certain disorder; *Cosmic Fork*, using the same process, rearranges blacks and whites. A last remark about torn paper: in the Cubist period, after the first glued paper, there had appeared in the painting of Braque and Picasso certain canvases in which the painting itself imitated the glued paper in trompe l'œil. In the same way, Arp sometimes undertook works "in the aftermath of torn paper" in which the oil forms painted on cardboard imitated the appearance of torn paper, as if Arp himself were mocking his own process.

As Arp became notorious, he began to receive commissions. Among the books and the illustrated albums, *Eleven Painters Viewed By Arp* (1949), and *Dreams and Projects* should be noted because of their beautiful woodcuts. Among the public commissions, the most significant is without a doubt the monumental work for UNESCO. In 1950, Arp executed a vast mural relief for the Graduate Center at Harvard: his native city paid him homage in 1953, and it was doubtlessly in 1954 that the most important recognition was granted: he received the international prize for sculpture given by the Biennale. His joy must have been even greater because of the fact that two of his old friends were honored at the same time: Max Ernst received the prize for painting and Joan Miró, that for graphic arts. This triple prize marked the triumph of Surrealism, but André Breton, who was not consulted, revolted against the idea that a Surrealist could accept a prize. Curiously, he blames Max Ernst, but he spares Arp. In 1959, Breton was to go as far as to award in his own way the absolute prize for Surrealism to Arp for his preface to the Salon of May "which constitutes the most authorized and the most pure professions of *Surrealist* faith.'' Italics are Breton's.

THE LAST YEARS

In 1956, Arp was seventy years old. Other recognition in the form of prizes, invitations and public commissions would come from around the world. But in the threshold of old age, Arp was not the kind of man who would feel as if he had "made it." He was to take his study of form even further and to develop those forms he had discovered. Several examples will illustrate this.

Arp's reputation as a sculptor of typical forms, rounded and marvelously polished, is well-established. He

Hannah Höch, Hans Richter, Juliette Man Ray, X, Man Ray in front of a tapestry of S. Taeuber, Düsseldorf, 1958.

would continue to do beautiful sculptures: *Nude with Buds, Cloud Goblet, Cloud Animal* (1961), *Galaxy Tear, Woman Landscape* (1962), *Torso Leaf, The Outskirt Saint* (1963) and *Delightful Nest* (1965). In his last years, he wanted to multiply the exceptions. A sculpture like *Geometrical-Ageometrical* (1940), in which a round element is sunken into an angular, rectilinear solid, remains uncommon. Brusquely contrasting forms would not be rare: *Chesspiece* (1958) is an enormous curvilinear figure on a double base, unstable but with clean angles (could this reference to chess be an homage to a game which his old friends Duchamp, Tzara, Richter and Man Ray were so enthusiastic?). Like the Greek mythology to which Arp was not afraid to refer, *Daphne II* (1960), is a feminine torso transformed into a tree whose crown and branches have been cut; the rectitude of the cuts is even more accentuated by the angular pseudo-base on which it rests; the angle seems to be forced into a cube that would have given under the blow of the lumberjack artist. *Geometric Flat-Band Goblet* (1962) is a square block of curvilinear cross-sections on which are placed three unusual geometrical solid forms. *Scanning the Horizon* (1964) recalls the structure of *Three Superimposed Goblets*, but here only one element retains the majority of its rounded forms. In 1964 and 1965, three or four geometrical structures appeared, squat, cast in one piece, like *Eye of the Tower* (1965), *Yawning Shell* (1965), or the singular *Doll Seesaw* (1964), a sort of open pliers oscillating on a curved base; without the discreet presence on each side of the pliers of two symmetrical oblong reliefs in which the ''dolls'' can be discerned and recognized as being of the same period, the sculpture would not be recognizable as Arp's.

In two types of works, Arp abandoned the flat, smooth surface of his sculptures. On the one hand, two statuettes were simply kneaded, of which perhaps too much has been made even though the technique was not continued: *Triers Landscape* and *Triers Man-Tower* (1961); on the other hand, in a numerous series of *Forest-Wheels* (1961), large circular granite stones, a meter in diameter, were pierced in the center with a varying cut. On at least one of their faces, Arp left raw stone, in all of its roughness, with all of its grain (in this instance, the versions in bronze are less convincing than those in stone). These stones do not

have a completely ''sculpted'' air, as Arp imagines them in the forest or at least in vegetation. They can be rolled, their positions changed and the position of the motif in their center varied. Herbert Read realized that this form not only has an esthetic *raison d'être:* ''Arp had always liked to see his sculptures in a natural environment. Toward the end of his life, in his garden in Tessin, he sculpted large circular stone slabs as if they were grindstones, pierced by his characteristic motifs. They had this shape so that they could be rolled from one position to another, in order to be able to vary the natural environment from time to time.'' This was one way of not freezing the work and of introducing something into it independent of the will of the artist. Sculpture is even more changeable when one of its faces is polite and the other is not.

One series in particular appeared in 1959-60, that of the *Heads*, of which there are at least three versions. The *Helmet Heads* are slightly pointed ovals posed on a base, where the placement of an eventual face is anticipated by a gentle undulation. *Drawer Head* is a bit more humorous; it has a helmet-like form, but there is no incipient ''face''; on the contrary, a transversal cut makes a geometric block in the shape of a trapezoid which opens like a drawer, leaving a hollow on one side where there is a protrusion on the other, without resorting to *trompe l'oeil* effects like those of the figurative Surrealists.

In the second half of the 'twenties, Arp had done some sculptural reliefs, flat structures of an equal thickness that were able to sustain themselves on a base. Then, sculpture in the round seemed to have deflected him from these intermediary works between sculpture and relief. But later, he went back to this form and derived many unusual effects from it. A few examples will be cited here. *The Little Theater* (1959) is on a background of an irregular rectangle from which an irregular square is cut, in which appear two new elements that suggest puppets in a theater. In *Undulating Threshold* (1960), there is no longer a way to place the sculpture; it is a massive elegant form with two hollows and without an identifiable base (one could just place it flatly on the ground), while in *Initial of a Leaf* (1960), there is still a rectilinear base that can be used or ignored. In both cases, the sculpture has multiple positions. *Dancing Ceremony* (1960) has only one position, upright, because of the bounding dancer's form it suggests; but its extremely nimble forms bounding through space make one forget that this is a flat sculpture: its lack of profile is an element of surprise.

Arp would combine this return of interest in the sculpture relief with themes and forms he had recently imagined. Thus, *Banner-Wheel* (1962) is an oval in which a large empty form is hollowed out. One thinks of the *Forest-Wheels* of the same period; like them, *Banner-Wheel* has a single position. These flat sculptures would also lend themselves to research in symmetry to which Arp was about to dedicate himself in *Sculpture Column* (1961), *One-eyed Warrior* (1965) and *Inverted Columns* (1965), among other works.

Since creating certain woodcuts and the sculptures from the height of Dada, Arp was only rarely interested in symmetry. He returned to it in his graphic work and sculpture in the 'sixties. There are several cases of figures like this that are manifested first in experiences with tapering columns ranging from *Nude with Buds* (1961) to

27

Torso-Vase (1963) and including the *Daphnes*, which conspicuously reject symmetry. In *Sculpture-Column* (1961), a totally upright form in duralumin, a light metal that requires only a small base, the symmetry is perfect: an infinite undulation or a feminine form carrying a pitcher on its head, with such an upward movement that one forgets it is a relief sculpture, flat, and not a column. Smaller and more compact, the *One-eyed Warrior* (1965) also assumes perfect symmetry. During these same years, Arp became interested in oblong forms, vaguely humanoid, that he was to call "dolls" from time to time; several collages, therefore, bear this name. The dolls are to be found in sculpture and even more so in the round, whether in perfect symmetry or in single-plane symmetry, as in the strange *One-eyed Doll* (1963) with a sole protruding eye and half of the body simply bulged out. In many other sculptures, Arp gives the impression that he was interested in altering symmetry. *Star Amphora* (1965) would have been a perfect amphora if a double horizontal section had not been taken away, separating the neck from the body by another fragment moved out of place with respect to the central axis; this fragment is foreign to the spirit of the otherwise perfectly symmetrical amphora, unless there is a fragment missing; it is easy to get lost in conjecture about these disrupted lines and volumes. More disorienting to the eye, at first glance, is *Inverted Columns* (1965). A flat form undulates irregularly, separated into two parts in its center along a perpendicular axis well marked by a space left between the two elements; only a more attentive look can perceive the oblique symmetry: a column cut into two absolutely similar and symmetrical forms, whose symmetry is camouflaged because they have been placed head to tail.

Arp never abandoned his taste for fun in any of his activities. He continued to surprise in different ways in

his reliefs. *Concrete Relief* of 1961, in duralumin, has an atypically narrow format. But *Page from a Floral Book* (1960), with a more common format, is in cardboard painted with oil in which the principal motif inscribed in a yellow and white rectangle, completely decentered, seems to be sunken into its frame. Care must be taken not to forget Arp's reliefs without support, generally in small formats (20 to 30 centimeters), called *découpages*, of which he would make several dozen copies. Planned without support, these metallic découpages could be placed flat or hung on a background of color, or even on a transparent background like Plexiglas.

The collages of this period are equally free: simple black forms are inscribed in a white circle (*Collage*, 1964), or, more complex, the cut fragments mix with the torn ones (*Collages*, 1964). We have already mentioned the dolls, painted, collé or sculpted; but Arp also used the collage, like the aquarelle and other techniques, to accomplish a monumental project or tapestry. He prepared, in effect, a certain number of tapestry designs on the subject of his own death (*The Siege of the Air, Phantom Stairway*, 1961; *Bird Door*, posthumously completed) or related subjects (*Curtain*, 1960), as well as diverse objects: dishes, jewels and even liturgical objects.

As in the past, when Arp looked for something new, he thought first of paper. In the 'sixties, that produced new ink designs, several beautiful aquarelles and crayon drawings in which the paper was rubbed and delicately shaded. In a small number of paintings, among his last (1964-66), it is surprising that there are no longer uniform flat surfaces, and one finds an uncharacteristic Expressionist touch. It was in this style that Arp painted, undoubtedly in 1965, his *Last Self-portrait*, hurriedly brushed in oil: something between a carnival mask smiling beneath a large nose and round eyes and a raw work of art. Thus, humor has the last word.

Arp's last years were happy and productive. All of his poems in German and his writings in French were collected. He even had the pleasure of seeing some of his poems set to music by good composers, Wladimir Vogel and Sean O. Riada. Arp was a celebrity, fêted a bit almost everywhere in the world. The Paris Musée d'Art Moderne dedicated a retrospective exposition to him in 1962, organized by Jean Cassou. Arp had been worrying about something since the time of Taeuber's death. He had imagined that her works could be preserved along with his in a foundation. Throughout the 'sixties, this idea became more urgent to him, and Arp, aided by his advisers, undertook its implementation. After his death, it was Marguerite Hagenbach, encouraged by François Arp, who achieved the final legal and material establishment of the foundation, which has as its center the house in Meudon constructed by Taeuber; there is also an equivalent in Germany, in Rolandseck. Under the care of people who respected and loved the Arps, the center conserves archives and information about Arp and Taeuber, accessible to artists and amateurs wishing to know their work better. It is an active place whose goal is "to collect, to increase, and to make accessible on a world wide scale the work of Jean Arp and Sophie Taeuber-Arp"; but, according to its statutes, "the foundation should, in addition, promote and favor, through the aid of its funds, the activity of artists in the world." So that this place may always be alive for art, young artists

Denise René and Arp. Exhibition of 1962. Photo A. Morain

Arp in his garden, Meudon. Photo A. Morain

are regularly invited to install their studios in what was Arp's. Arp's sculptures are placed on the grass, on stairways, in gravel paths, or on walls, in natural, welcoming situations, as the artist wished.

A particular link between France, Germany and Switzerland, the Arp-Taeuber Foundation is in fact an artistic space that transcends the boundaries of language and culture, being more universal than international. It is not necessary to insist on the importance that should be accorded a collection of an artist's works, assembled by the artist himself in the same place where he lived, constituting unique creations that he did not wish to let pass from his own property, original models and copies conserved for his own pleasure, especially if a certain number of them are conserved as he had wished and placed in the environment he desired. Thus, it was for many reasons that this book is based on works preserved at the foundation, to which a great part of the photographs and information concerning dates, dimensions and locations of works by Arp are owed.

"Suppressing frontiers leads to the essential," wrote Arp in *Unsern täglichen Traum*. It is true that few artists have overcome frontiers as much as Arp did. Through his personal history and philosophy, he transcended not only political, linguistic and cultural frontiers, but also esthetic frontiers between conventional genres (reliefs are not exactly sculpture, nor painting; the torn paper, not exactly collage, etc.). And yet, from all of his force and all of his art, the frontiers between the elements of reality and of the imaginary, in whom besides Arp could the blending of a wheel and a forest take place without hiatus, without frenzy, without disorder, and for the pleasure of the eyes and of the spirit? A mirror and an echo? A woman and a landscape? Where birds can use doors and masks, or the contrary? Where does the cosmos use forks, and stars amphoras? Where is it natural to see concretions intertwine? Where can a hat be heard to purr? This oeuvre is nothing less than a great appeal to freedom. There are, of course, other ways of achieving freedom, but Arp's achievement is accomplished without weapons and without inconvenient agitations.

In the last text of the large collective book *Jours effeuillés*, which was published as a foreword to an exhibition he was doing with his friend Richter — the last one he did in the Galerie Denise René while still alive — Arp states: "To be full of joy when looking at an oeuvre is not a little thing" (JE, p. 571). In a time as dominated by confusion as our own, and which privileges the pathetic in art and life, the tragic or the sarcastic and the grimacing, a case in which calm joy — a joy produced while regarding one's own oeuvre — is not to be taken lightly. Artists like Arp, after all, do not come along that frequently.

CHRONOLOGY

1886. Hans Peter Wilhelm Arp is born September 16, 1886. His father, Jürgen Wilhelm Arp (1853-1921), is German and his mother, Marie-Joséphine Koeberlé (1857-1929), is Alsatian; they run a cigar factory and live at 52, rue du Vieux Marché aux Poissons.

1891. Hans' brother Franz, normally called Willie, is born. The two brothers will always be very close and friendly throughout their lives. They are trilingual, speaking German, French and the Alsatian dialect.

1893. Hans starts to show a great interest in drawing, particularly during the holidays he spends in a country house owned by his parents in Grendelbruch in the Vosges. However, he turns out to be a poor student, adapting badly to the Prussian disciplinary code of the school.

1896. Arp starts his secondary education and does so poorly that his father has to hire a private tutor, Henri Meyer, who would not oppose the artistic tastes of his pupils. Arp develops a passion for the German Romantics. He paints, draws, writes poems and tries wood sculpture. He starts a long friendship with his classmates René Schwaller and Lucien Neitzel.

1900. Arp enters the Strasbourg Arts and Crafts School but loses interest the following year.

1901. He studies drawing with the young painter Georges Ritleng.

1902. Through Georges Ritleng, Arp contacts the poets of *Der Stürmer* magazine, which publishes nine ussues in 1902: Otto Flake, René Schickelé, Ernst Stadler and Albert Mathies, who wrote in the Alsatian dialect. Arp's first poem would be published in Alsatian.

1903. Arp's first poem, illustrated by himself, is published in *Hazweiess*. Always friendly with Ritleng, Schickelé, Flake and Stadler, he publishes his first poem in German in the ephemeral magazine *Der Stänkerer*. He draws, paints and sculpts.

1904. Arp visits Paris for the first time and stays with a maternal uncle. He is enthusiastic about the city, its atmosphere and its museums. He would like to study there, but his father prefers to send him to the Weimar Fine Arts Academy. He registers at Weimar in November.

1905. At the Weimar Academy, Arp meets Henri Van de Velde and Count Harry Kessler. He starts a friendship with a young painter, Ivo Hauptmann. Arp is impressed by an exhibition of sculptures by Maillol. He paints in a Neo-Impressionist style. In a poetical anthology published in Strasbourg, his poems are published side by side with those of Stadler and Schickelé in *Zeitgenössische Dichtung des Elsasses*, appearing as "a real epigone of the *Der Stürmer*." During holidays with his family in Grendelbruch, he paints a fresco with Ritleng, a mixture of Art Nouveau and pseudo-Egyptian style.

1906. His father must leave Alsatia for reasons of health. The Arp family moves to Weggis, near Lucerne. Arp would work there in great solitude.

1907. Thanks to a recommendation by Van de Velde, Arp exhibits at the Bernheim Jeune Gallery in Paris, with Matisse, Signac and Van Dongen.

1908. Arp registers at the Julian Academy. His friends in Paris are, of course, Ritleng and Hauptmann, but also Oscar Lüthy, Wilhelm Gimmi and Walter Helbig.

1909-10. In the solitude of Weggis, Arp paints large canvases, so abstract that they meet only with incomprehension. Only the painter Baranoff-Rossiné encourages him. He is introduced to plaster techniques by the sculptor Fritz Huf.

1911. Arp, Lüthy and Helbig found *Der Moderne Bund*, a group of painters which organizes an exhibition in the Hôtel du Lac in Lucerne (Amiet, Arp, Friesz, Gauguin, Gimmi, Helbig, Herbin, Huber, Klee, Lüthy, Matisse, Picasso).

1912. Arp meets Kandinsky and participates in the elaboration of the *Almanach der Blaue Reiter* and in the second exhibition of the group in Munich. *Der Moderne Bund* organizes its second exhibition in Zurich. Arp is in contact from then on with the international avant-garde.

1913. *Der Moderne Bund* exhibits in Munich and in Berlin. Arp establishes contact with the *Der Sturm* gallery and magazine, in which he would collaborate. He publishes *Die Neue Französische Malerei*, an album which presents the new tendencies in French painting from Rousseau to Picasso.

1914-15. During a stay in Cologne, Arp meets the painters of the *Rheinischen Expressionisten* group: August Macke, Heinrich Nauen and, above all, Max Ernst, with whom he would have a great friendship. When war is declared, he flees to Paris with his brother. He lives in Montmartre and frequently sees Apollinaire, Picasso, Max Jacob, Modigliani, Herbin and Eggeling. He decorates a theosophic institute for his friend René Schwaller and does a series of illustrations for the *Bhagavad Gita*. Lack of resources and bureaucratic harassment force the two brothers to flee to Switzerland in May 1915.

1915. In Switzerland, Arp first goes to see Arthur Segal in Ascona. He works with Otto and Adya van Rees, a Dutch artist couple, and the three of them exhibit together in the Tanner Gallery in Zurich. It is in this exhibition that Arp meets Sophie Taeuber, whose personality seduces him. He does an abstract fresco with Otto van Rees in the Pestalozzi School in Zurich.

1916. In the beginning of February, the poet Hugo Ball founds the Cabaret Voltaire, where Arp, Tzara, Janco and Huelsenbeck join him immediately. Dada is born one way or another. From then on, they would be the pillars and the leaders of the movement, to be joined later by Richter, Serner and several other local and foreign poets and artists. This radical and cosmopolitan avant-garde overwhelms the public. Arp and Taeuber begin works in collaboration, although Taeuber's main interest is dance, which she studies at the Laban School; before long, they would be living together.

1917. More and more provocative shows and events take place in the Cabaret Voltaire. Arp writes poetry and creates collages, reliefs, woodcuts and illustrations for the magazine *Dada* and for books by his friends Tzara and Huelsenbeck. Ball and his companion, Emmy Hennings, retire to the Tessin after the closing of the cabaret. But the Dada Gallery is immediately opened and would be from then on the scene of the principal Dada events, which are to take an even more provocative turn.

1918. Dada begins to spread beyond Switzerland. Arp signs the manifesto of the Berlin Dadaists. He meets Picabia and Gabrielle Buffet. Tzara publishes his *Dada Manifesto 1918*. Arp participates in the activities of the Zurich Dadaists, and in other exhibitions as well.

1919. In the Dada soirée in the Kaufleuten Hall in Zurich, Arp is one of the main protagonists, notably in the décors of the ballet *Noir Cacadou*. He collaborates on the *Anthologie dada* and in the magazine *Der Zeltweg*. He establishes contact with Max Ernst and Theodor Baargeld, who have founded a Dada group in Cologne.

1920. Arp does a series of *Fatagaga* works with Max Ernst. In the Winter Brewery in Cologne, the Dada exhibition organized by Ernst, Baargeld and Arp causes a scandal. Arp participates in the Dada Fair in Berlin as well. He publishes woodcuts and poetry (*Die Wolkenpumpe* and *Der Vogel Selbdritt*). In Paris, Arp meets Breton, Soupault, Aragon and Ribemont-Dessaignes, who, after the arrival of Picabia and Tzara, organize boisterous Dada events.

1921. Arp participates in the Dada Salon in the Montaigne Gallery in Paris. He visits the Futurists in Rome. During the summer, he goes to the Tyrol with Ernst, Tzara and Éluard and publishes *Dada au grand air* with them. He illustrates *Le passager du transatlantique*, by Benjamin Péret.

1922. Arp travels extensively. He collaborates in several avant-garde magazines. He organizes a festival in the Bauhaus, where he sees Tzara, Richter, Schwitters, van Doesburg, El Lissitzky and Moholy-Nagy again. He is married to Sophie Taeuber.

1923. Arp stays with Schwitters in Hanover. Schwitters publishes his collection *7 Arpaden*. He is denied Swiss nationality.

1924. Arp collaborates on several magazines and publishes *Der Pyramidenrock*. He joins the Surrealists. Breton publishes his *Manifeste du Surréalisme*.

1925. Not having obtained a visa, Arp is forced to leave Switzerland. He participates in the first Surrealist Exhibition in the Loeb Gallery. He does not frequent the Surrealist meetings, but he does sign the group's manifestos and publishes in their magazines. He publishes *Die Kunstismen* in collaboration with Lissitzky. During a trip to Italy, he reencounters Hugo Ball and Emmy Hennings.

1926. Arps opts for French nationality. In Strasbourg, where he is staying with his brother, he is asked to decorate the Aubette. He undertakes the work with Taeuber and van Doesburg. Taeuber finishes plans for the house they are to build on terrain they bought in Meudon-Val-Fleury, in an enclave of Clamart.

1927. Arp becomes friendly with Michel Seuphor. He has a one-man show in the Surrealist Gallery, presented by André Breton.

1928. The Aubette opens in Strasbourg. Arp exhibits in Brussels with other Surrealist artists.

1929. Arp travels to Brittany with the Delaunays. He joins Seuphor's and Torres Garcia's group Cercle et Carré. The magazine *Variétés* publishes two reproductions of sculpture in the round by Arp. The Arps move into the house at Meudon.

1930. Arp participates in the exhibition of the Cercle et Carré group without its affecting his relations with the Surrealists. He participates in an exhibition of collages for which Aragon writes *La peinture au défi*. He publishes *Weiszt du schwarzt du*, illustrated by Max Ernst, and *Konfiguration*.

1931. Arp joins the Abstraction-Creation group with Taeuber. He collaborates on the magazine *Transition*. He writes *Trois nouvelles exemplaires* in French with Vicente Huidobro.

1932. Arp participates in exhibits, the most important of which are in Basel and Lodz. Arp and Taeuber join the writing staff of the magazine *Abstraction-Création*. Arp does his first torn-paper works.

1933. Arp does the "Human Concretion" series. He collaborates on the Surrealist magazines *Le surréalisme au service de la révolution* and *Minotaure*.

1934. In June, Arp and Sophie Taeuber break with Abstraction-Creation and are on bad terms with Christian Zervos.

1936. Arp participates in the New York exhibitions "Cubism and Abstract Art" and "Fantastic Art, Dada and Surrealism" and collaborates on the English magazine *Axis*. He participates in the first Surrealist exhibition in London.

1937. Arp publishes *Des taches dans le vide*, his first collection of poems in French. The magazine *Plastique* is published, edited by Sophie Taeuber and Cesar Domela.

1938. Arp publishes his second collection in French, *Sciure de gamme*. He participates in the International Surrealist Exhibition at the Beaux Arts Gallery in Paris.

1939. Arp participates in the collective novel *L'homme qui a perdu son squelette*, which appears in *Plastique*. He changes his name to Jean. Arp and Taeuber exhibit their work at the Jeanne Bucher Gallery. Arp publishes *Muscheln und Schirme*, poetry in German.

1940. Just before the occupation of Paris, the Arps flee to Dordogne, where they meet Gabrielle Buffet and Domela. They then go to Peggy Guggenheim's in Annecy and finally establish themselves in Grasse with the Magnellis. A number of Surrealists go to Marseille to try to get an American visa. Arp devotes himself to sculpture.

1941. *Poèmes sans prénoms*, in French, a collection illustrated by Taeuber, is published. Sonia Delaunay joins Arp and the Magnellis. The little community of artists does a series of lithographs collectively.

1942. Arp and Taeuber's situation becomes more precarious, and, unable to obtain an American visa, they take refuge in Switzerland.

1943. Taeuber dies of asphyxiation from the fumes of a coal stove. Arp is crushed and slows down his activities. He spends several weeks in a Dominican cloister.

1944. Arp publishes *Rire de coquille* in German and French, dedicated to the memory of Taeuber. He exhibits in New York.

1945. Arp returns to Paris. Max Bill publishes his *Eleven Configurations*. From then on, Arp would share life with a friend from Basel, Marguerite Hagenbach, who had collected his work for several years.

1946. *Siège de l'air*, a collection of poems in French illustrated with duo-drawings by Arp and Taeuber, is published. Arp exhibits for the first time at Denise René's, which was to be his principal gallery. He goes back to work at his studio in Meudon.

1947. Arp starts to sculpt again. He participates in the International Surrealist Exhibition at the request of Breton and Duchamp.

1948. A selection of poems and essays, *On My Way*, is published in New York, and in Zurich, *Onze peintres vus par Arp* is published.

1949. Arp goes to the United States for the first time; he sees his friends Huelsenbeck, Richter and Duchamp.

1950. Arp takes another trip to the United States at the invitation of Walter Gropius; he does a monumental relief at the Graduate Student Center at Harvard. He has exhibitions in the Maeght Gallery, at the Denise René Gallery in Paris and at the Sidney Janis Gallery in New York. He publishes *Souffle et Elément*, poetry and woodcuts.

1951. *Jalons* and *Auch das ist nur eine Wolke* are published.

1952. *Rêves et projets* and *Die Engelschrift*, a poem to Taeuber, are published. Hans Richter shoots a sequence of his film *Dreams that Money Can Buy* with Arp. Arp takes a trip to Greece.

1953. Arp publishes two books of poetry, *Wortträume und schwarze Sterne* and *Behaarte Herzen 1923-1928 Könige vor der Sintflut 1952-53*. He creates a monumental sculpture, *Berger de nuages*, for the University of Caracas. There is an exhibition in his home town.

1954. Arp is awarded the international grand prix for sculpture at the Biennale of Venice.

1955. *Auf einem Bein* and *Unsern täglichen Traum* are published. Arp makes his second trip to Greece.

1956. Arp and Schwitters hold a joint exhibition in Bern.

1957. *Worte mit und ohne Anker* and *Le voilier dans la forêt*, poetry with woodcuts in color, are published. Arp does *Constellation*, a monumental relief for UNESCO. His first catalog of sculptures is compiled by C. Giedion-Welcker and M. Hagenbach.

1958. An Arp retrospective is held at the Museum of Modern Art in New York. Arp makes a trip to the United States and Mexico. There are numerous exhibitions of his work throughout the world.

1959. Arp publishes an album of engravings, an album of silkscreen prints and *Mondsand*, a book of poetry. He marries Marguerite Hagenbach in Basel; they buy the villa Ronco dei Fiori in Solduno, near Locarno.

1960. *Zweiklang, Sophie Taeuber-Arp, Hans Arp* and *Vers le blanc infini* are published. Arp goes to Egypt and the Middle East; in Israel, he meets his old friend Marcel Janco. He creates a monumental relief in aluminium for the École technique in Brauschweig.

1961. Arp publishes *Sinnende Flammen*, poetry. He does stele and reliefs in concrete for the École des arts appliquées of Basel. He travels to the Rhine and Moselle valleys. The first *Forest-Wheels* are created.

1962. A traveling retrospective of Arp's work is organized by the Musée National d'Art Moderne of Paris.

1963. The first volume of Arp's collected poems in German, *Gesammelte Gedichte*, is published. He receives the National Prize for the Arts. He does several sacred objects.

1964. Arp is awarded the Carnegie Prize and the Nordrhein-Westfallen Grand Prix for Sculpture.

1965. *L'ange et la rose* and *Logbuch des Traumkapitäns* are published. An enlargement of *Hommage to Rodin* is placed in the Place de Strasbourg and *Scanning the Horizon* in a square in The Hague. The Arp-Richter exhibition in the Denise René Gallery is the last Arp will attend.

1966. *Soleil recerclé*, poems and woodcuts in color, are published. The fiftieth anniversary of Dada is celebrated by placing a relief by Arp in the alleyway in which the Cabaret Voltaire had been located. Marcel Jean collects a large volume of writings in French by Arp, *Jours Effeuillés*, which will appear the day after his death. Arp dies on June 7 of a heart attack. He is buried in the Locarno cemetery; one of his sculptures, *Star*, is placed on his tomb.

We express our gratitude to Greta Ströh, from the Arp Foundation, and to Denise René for their encouragement and for their invaluable assistance in obtaining our collection of illustrations.

SUCCINCT BIBLIOGRAPHY

MAJOR WRITINGS BY ARP

Worttraüme und schwarze Sterne. Wiesbaden: Limes Verlag, 1953.

Unsern täglichen Traum.... Zurich: Verlag der Arche, 1955.

Zweiklang: Sophie Täuber-Arp. Hans Arp. Zurich: Verlag der Arche, 1960.

Gesammelte Gedichte I, 1903-1939. Zurich: Verlag der Arche, Wiesbaden: Limes Verlag, 1963.

Jours Effeuillés. Paris: Gallimard, 1966.

Gesammelte Gedichte II, 1939-1957. Zurich: Verlag der Arche, Wiesbaden: Limes Verlag, 1984.

Logbuch, bilingual edition, translated by A. Bleikasten. Paris: Artfuyen, 1983.

Gesammelte Gedichte III, 1957-1966. Zurich: Verlag der Arche, Wiesbaden: Limes Verlag, 1984.

With R. Huelsenbeck. *Dada in Zurich*. Zurich: Sanssouci, 1957.

CATALOGS AND BIBLIOGRAPHIES

WILHELM F. ARNTZ. *Arp. Das graphische Werk*. La Haye, 1980.

AIMÉE BLEIKASTEN. *Arp. Bibliographie*. London, 1981-83, two volumes.

CAROLA GIEDION-WELCKER. *Hans Arp*. Stuttgart: Gerd Hatje, 1957.

BERND RAU. *Hans Arp. Die Reliefs*. Stuttgart: Gerd Hatje, 1981.

EDUARD TRIER. *Jean Arp. Sculptures 1957-1966*. Teufen: Niggli, 1968.

ON ARP

HUGO BALL. *Die Flucht aus der Zeit*. Lucerne: Stocker, 1946.

PETER BEYE and ST. VON WIESE. *Stiftung Marguerite Arp*. Stuttgart: Staatsgalerie, 1975.

GABRIELLE BUFFET-PICABIA. *Rencontres*. Paris: Belfond, 1977.

JEAN CATHELIN. *Arp*. Paris: Fall 1959.

REINHARD DÖHL. *Das Literarische Werk Hans Arps 1903-1930*. Stuttgart: Metzlersche Verlagsbuchhandlung, 1967.

IONEL JIANOU. *Jean Arp*. Paris: Arted Éditions d'Art, 1973.

H. W. LAST. *Hans Arp the Poet of Dadaism*. London: Wolf, 1969.

GIUSEPPE MARCHIORI. *Arp. Cinquante ans d'activité*. Milan: Alfieri, 1964.

STEFANIE POLEY. *Hans Arp. Die Formensprache im plastischen Werk*. Stuttgart, 1978.

HERBERT READ. *Arp*. London: Thames and Hudson, 1968.

HANS RICHTER. *Dada: Kunst und Antikunst*. Cologne: DuMont Schauberg, 1964.

MICHEL SEUPHOR. *Arcadie d'Arp*. Paris: Hazan, 1957.

MICHEL SEUPHOR. *Arp*. Paris: Hazan, 1964.

GEORG SCHMIDT. *Sophie Taeuber-Arp*. Basel: Holbein, 1948.

MARGIT STABER. *Sophie Taeuber-Arp*. Lausanne: Rencontre, 1970.

TRISTAN TZARA. *Lampisteries Sept manifestes dada*. Paris: Pauvert, 1963.

ILLUSTRATIONS

PAINTINGS, GRAPHIC WORKS, COLLAGES, AND TORN PAPERS

1

1. *Self-portrait*, 1904-05.
Oil, 60×40 cm.
Fondation Arp-S. Taeuber, Rolandseck.

2. *Nude*, 1912.
Pencil, 26.5×15 cm.
Kunstmuseum, Basel.

3. *Drawing*, 1912.
Pencil, 30×23 cm.
Fondation Arp, Clamart.

4. *Three Women*, 1912.
Oil on canvas, 81×95 cm.
Fondation Arp, Clamart.

2

3

4

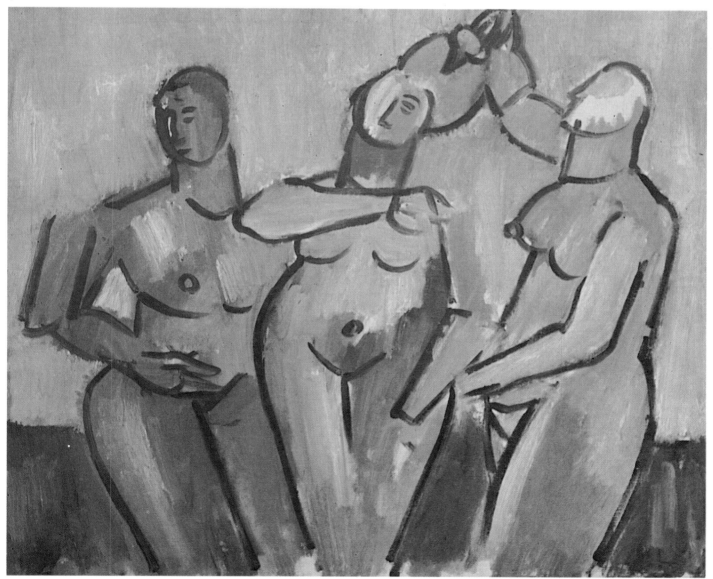

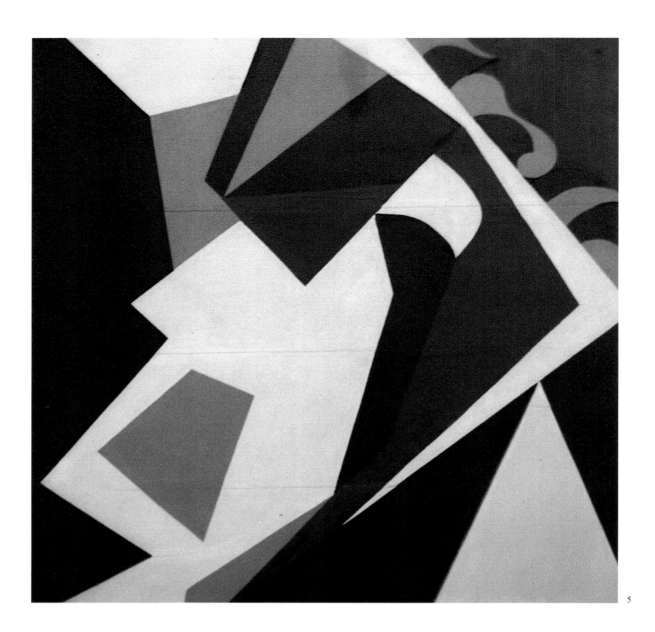

5

6

5. *Form*, 1914.
Painted wood, 120.5 × 120.5 cm.
Musée d'Art Moderne, Strasbourg.

6. *Crucifixion*, 1915.
India ink, 23 × 24 cm.
Fondation Arp, Clamart.

7. *Abstract Composition*, 1915.
Collage, 24 × 20 cm.
Kunstmuseum, Basel.

7

9

8

8. *Random Collage*, 1916.
Collage, 26 × 12.5 cm.
Musée de Bâle.

9. *India Ink*, 1918.
32 × 25.5 cm.
London Art Gallery.

10 & 11. *India Inks*, 1916.
27.4 × 21.2 cm
Arp Collection, Solduno.

12. *India Ink*, 1917.
34 × 26.2 cm.
Formerly in the Tzara Collection.

13. *India Ink*, 1917.
34 × 26.5 cm.
Formerly in the Tzara Collection.

10

11

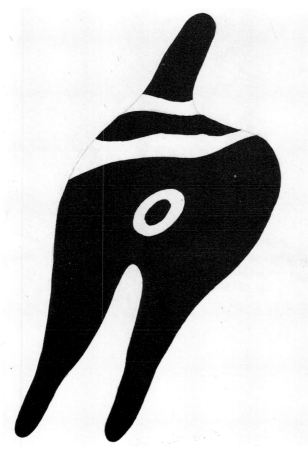

12

13

14

14. *Large Collage*, c. 1918.
96 × 76 cm.
Insel Hombroich Collection.

15. *Duo-Collage* (with Sophie Taeuber), 1918.
82 × 60 cm.
Insel Hombroich Collection.

16. *Ink on Tracing Paper*, 1919.
27.5 × 21 cm.
S. Collinet Collection.

17. *Wood Engraving* ("Der Zeltweg"), 1919.
24.5 × 18.5 cm.

18. *Drawing for the Dada Catalog*, 1919.
India ink, 22.4 × 19.6 cm.
Staatsgalerie Stuttgart.

19. *Drawing*, 1919.
India ink, 27 × 22 cm.
Whereabouts unknown.

15

16

17

18

19

20. *Figure-bust*, 1923.
Painted cutout cardboard, 31 × 22 cm.
S. Collinet Collection.

21. *Untitled*, c. 1925.
Oil, 75 × 106 cm.
Private Collection, Paris.

22. *The Priests of Florence*, 1927.
India ink and pencil, 22.3×26.8 cm.
Kunstmuseum, Basel.

23. *Frond and Navels*, 1926.
Painted scooped-out cardboard, 62×50 cm.
Fondation Arp-S. Taeuber, Rolandseck.

21

22

23

24

25

24. *Man, Moustache and Navel*, 1928 (1960).
Watercolor, 64 × 63.8 cm.
Fondation Arp, Clamart.

25. *Untitled*, 1930.
Gouache, 30.2 × 26 cm.
Private Collection.

26. *Second Torn Paper*, 1932.
28 × 22 cm.
Marguerite Arp-Hagenbach Collection.

27. *Torn Paper*, 1934.
37 × 37 cm.
Kunsthalle, Hamburg.

26

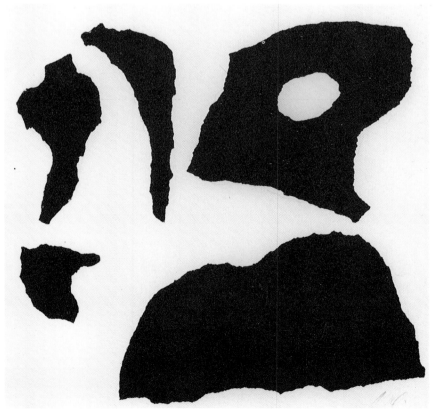

27

28. *Hand-Foot*, 1936.
India ink, 26.8×20.6.
Arp Collection, Basel.

29. *Vegetable Night*, 1938.
Torn drawing, 24.4×21.9 cm.
Private Collection, Basel.

30. *Torn Drawing*, 1938.
37.5×30 cm.
Fondation Arp, Clamart.

31. *Drawing with Fingers*, 1941.
India ink, 26.5×21 cm.
Kunstmuseum, Basel.

32. *Collage of Grasse*, 1941-42.
Torn photograph and gouache,
34.5×24.5 cm.
Fondation Arp, Clamart.

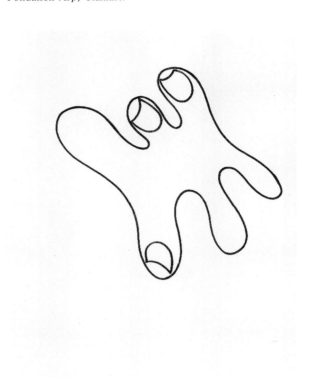

28

29

30

31

33. *India Ink*, 1941-42.
26.5×20.8 cm.
Awa Diarra-Ströh Collection, Clamart.

34. *Drawing with Fingers, Grasse*, 1941-42.
27.3×21 cm.
Fondation Arp-S. Taeuber, Rolandseck.

35. *India Ink*, 1941-42.
21×25 cm.
G. Ströh, Clamart.

36. *India Ink*, 1944.
31×23.5 cm.
Fondation Arp, Clamart.

35

33

34

36

48

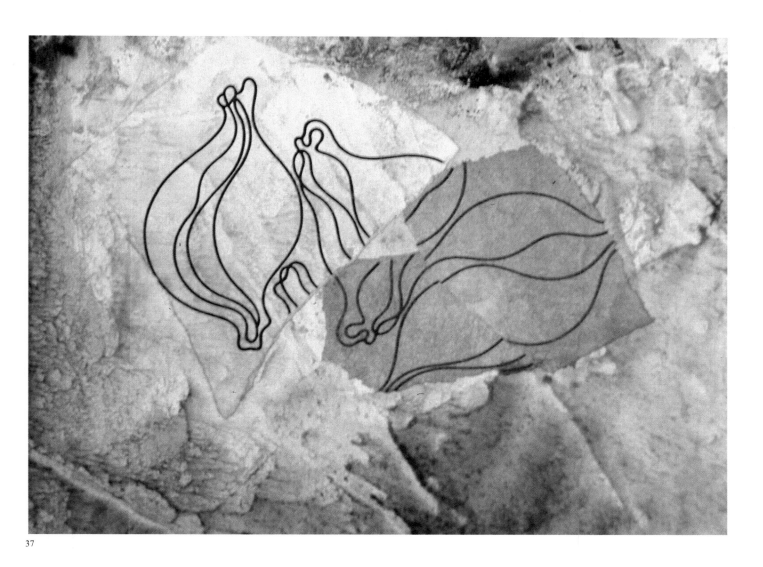

37

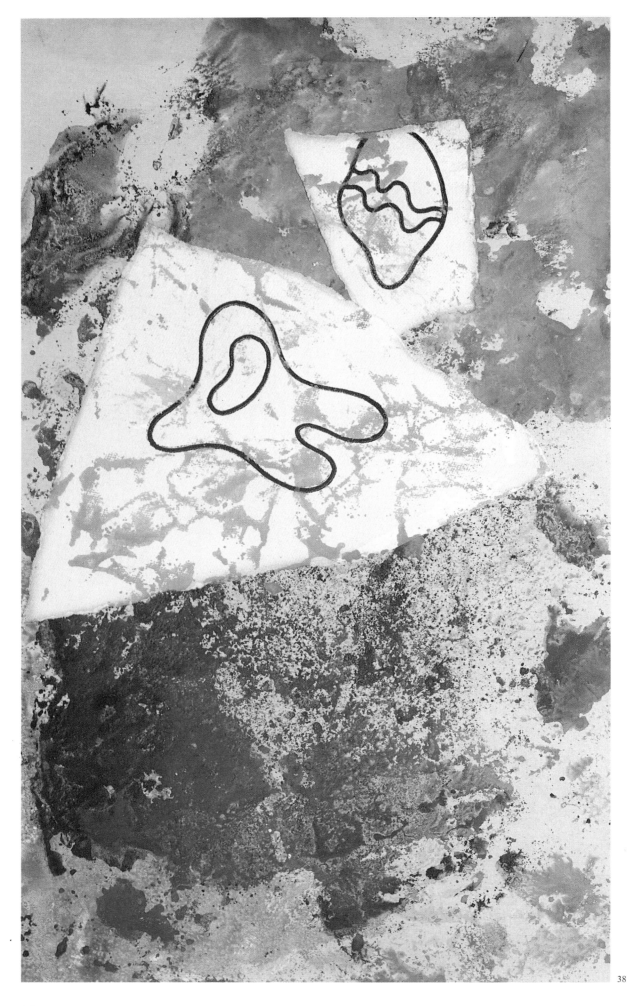

38. *Collage*, 1946.
30×18 cm.
Whereabouts unknown.

39. *Siamese Leaves*, 1949.
Engraving, Wash, 20.5×25 cm.
Victoria and Albert Museum, London.

40. *Preliminary Sketch for UNESCO*, 1950.
Gouache, 36×75.5 cm.
Galerie Denise René.

39

40

41

42

41. *Collage*, c. 1950.
Torn papers and gouache, 51 × 16 cm.
Whereabouts unknown.

42. *Head*, 1954.
Pencil, 27 × 21 cm.
Fondation Arp, Clamart.

43. *Torn Paper*, 1954.
Fragments of a 1920 work on wood, 25.4 × 19.4 cm.
Tate Gallery, London.

43

44. *Torn Paper*, 1950-53.
Collage from a photograph of
Sophie Taeuber's upholstery, 21 × 17.5 cm.
Fondation Arp, Clamart.

45. *Wings of the Forest*, 1955.
Gouache, 50 × 32.5 cm.
Arp Collection, Basel.

46. *Collage*, 1956.
49 × 14 cm.
Arp Collection, Solduno.

44

45

46

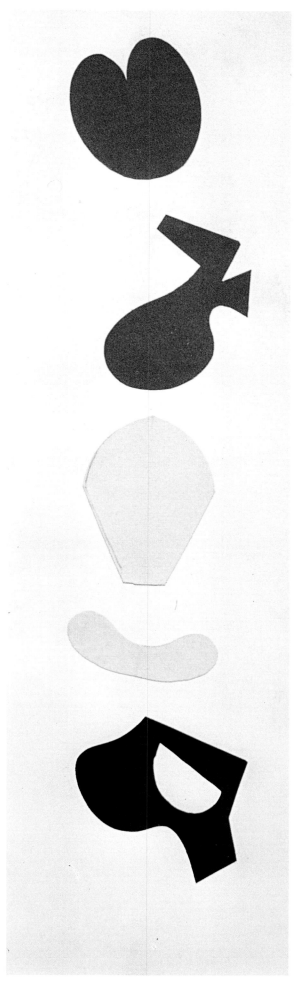

47. *Lightning Flash* (with M. Seuphor), 1956.
Torn drawing, 54×50 cm.
Fondation Arp-S. Taeuber, Rolandseck.

47

48. *Constellation of Five Forms*, 1956.
Gouache lithograph, 54.5 × 38.4 cm.
Formerly in the Hülbeck Collection.

49. *Crumpled paper*, 1958.
62 × 51 cm.
Fondation Arp, Clamart.

50. *Drawing*, 1958.
Crayon, 17.6 × 11.1 cm.
Fondation Arp, Clamart.

51. *Composition*, 1960.
Pencil, 60 × 40 cm.
Arp Collection, Solduno.

48

49

50

51

52

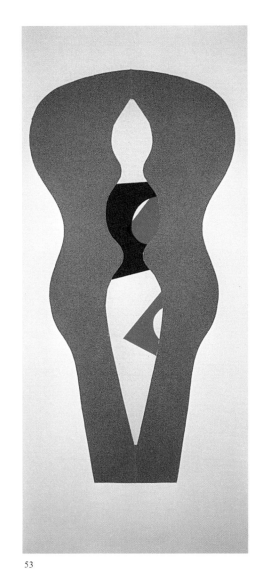

53

54

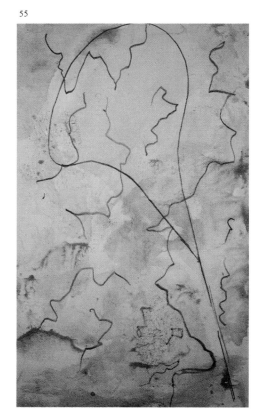

55

56

52. *Paints While Singing*, 1960.
Crumpled torn paper, 58 × 42.5 cm.
Private Collection.

53. *Doll*, 1962.
Collage, 59 × 25 cm.
Arp Collection, Solduno.

54. *Collage*, 1962.
33 × 33 cm.
Fondation Arp, Clamart.

55. *Watercolor Drawing*, 1963.
19 × 11 cm.
Hülbeck Collection.

56. *Watercolor Drawing*, c. 1963.
49.5 × 36 cm.
Hülbeck Collection.

57. *Interpreted Watercolor III*, 1963.
61 × 21 cm.
Fondation Arp, Clamart.

56

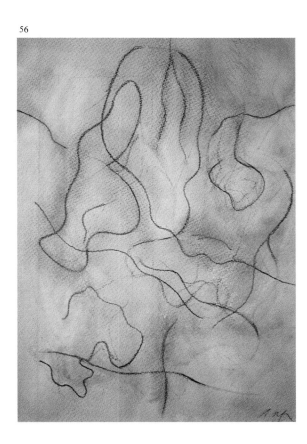

57

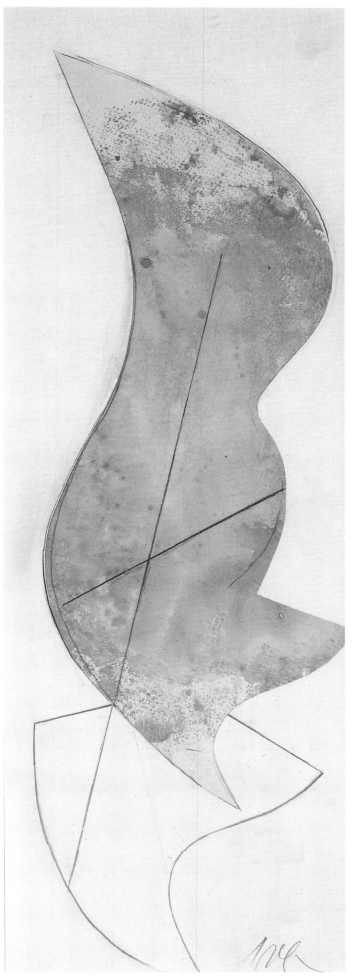

58. *Collage*, 1964.
63 × 50 cm.
Fondation Arp, Clamart.

59. *Doll Collage*, 1964.
37 × 17 cm.
Fondation Arp, Clamart.

60. *Encircled Sun*, 1962-65.
Collage, 25.3 × 21.3 cm.
J.L.P. Galleries, London.

61. *Last Self-portrait*, 1965.
Oil with original frame, 53.5 × 40 cm.
Fondation Arp-S. Taeuber, Rolandseck.

58

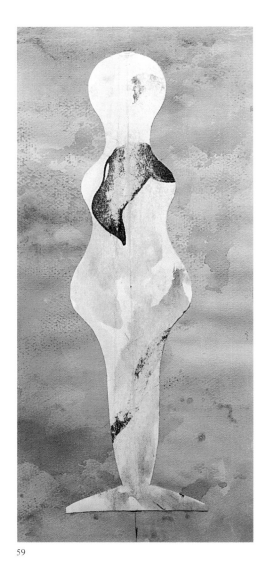

59

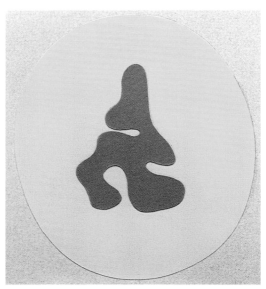

60

61

62. *Moon Dancer*, 1966.
Watercolor, 36.5×27 cm.
Dierdorf Collection, Lörrach.

62

63. The garden at Meudon-Clamart; in the background, Arp's studio.
From left to right: *The Outskirt Saint; Bird Skeleton; Demeter; Classical Sculpture.*

64. *Fruit of a Hand*, 1927-28.
Painted wood, 55 × 88 × 20 cm.
Kunsthaus, Zurich.

65. *Amphora* (with Sophie Taeuber), 1917.
Painted wood.
Height: 30 cm.
Fondation Arp, Clamart.

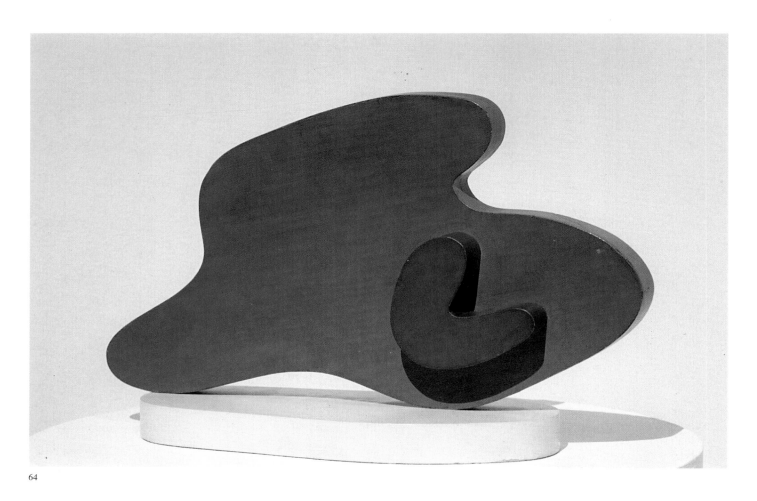

64

65

66. *Kaspar*, 1930.
Bronze, 50 × 28 × 19 cm.
Chalette Collection, New York.

67. *One Large and Two Small*, 1931.
Painted wood, 63 × 45 cm.
Fondation Arp, Clamart.

66

67

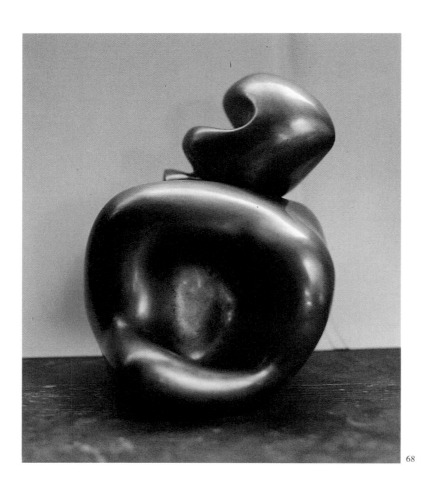

68

68. *Shell Head*, 1933.
Bronze, 20 × 25 × 18.5 cm.
Fondation Arp-S. Taeuber, Rolandseck.

69. *Pagoda Fruit*, 1934.
Cement, 23 × 33 × 38 cm.
Fondation Arp, Clamart.

70. *Human Concretion on Goblet*, 1935.
Bronze, 47 × 74 × 45.5 cm.
Fondation Arp, Clamart.

71. *Crown of Buds*, 1936.
Bronze, 52 × 42.5 × 42 cm.
Fondation Arp, Clamart.

69

70

71

72

73

72 & 73. *Moon Fruit*, 1936.
Stone, 110 × 150 × 100 cm.
Fondation Arp, Clamart.

74 & 75. *Seated*, 1937.
Bronze, 33 × 40 × 20 cm.
Fondation Arp, Clamart.

74

75

76

77

78

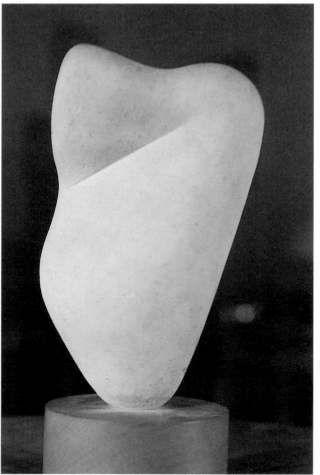

79

76. *Pre-Adamite Fruit*, 1938.
Bronze, 29.5 × 23.5 × 17 cm.
Fondation Arp, Clamart.

77. *Dreaming*, 1937.
Bronze, 37 × 20 × 21 cm.
Fondation Arp, Clamart.

78. *Homage to Rodin*, 1938-65.
Plaster, 27 × 22 × 11.5 cm.
Fondation Arp, Clamart.

79. *Owl Dream*, 1937-38.
Plaster, 26 × 15 × 13 cm.
Fondation Arp, Clamart.

80. *Milestone* (with Sophie Taeuber), 1938.
Wood, 60 × 25 × 36 cm.
Fondation Arp, Clamart.

80

81

81. *Mediterranean Sculpture I*, 1941.
Bronze, 38 × 27 × 16.5 cm.
Fondation Arp, Clamart.

82. *Mediterranean Group*, 1941-42.
Bronze, 21 × 35 × 17.5 cm.
Fondation Arp, Clamart.

83. *Geometrical-Ageometrical*, 1942.
Bronze, 30 × 28.5 × 16.5 cm.
Fondation Arp, Clamart.

82

83

84. *Superimposed Goblets*, 1947.
Bronze, 97 × 45 × 47 cm.
Fondation Arp, Clamart.

84

85. *Bird Skeleton*, 1947.
Bronze, 108 × 57 × 57 cm.
Fondation Arp, Clamart.

86. Another view of the same.

85

86

87. *Impish Shape*, 1949.
Bronze, 39 × 15 × 18 cm.
Fondation Arp, Clamart.

88 & 89. *Frond*, 1950.
Stone, 30 × 20.5 × 17.5 cm.
Fondation Arp, Clamart.

87

88

89

90. *Pistil*, 1950.
Cement, 88×40×36 cm.
Fondation Arp, Clamart.

91. *Mythical Figure*, 1950.
Bronze, 113×38.5×35 cm.
Fondation Arp, Clamart.

90

91

92. *Evocation of a Human,*
Moon-like, Ghostly Form, 1950.
Bronze, 28 × 22.5 × 17 cm.
Fondation Arp, Clamart.

93. *Howl*, 1951.
Bronze, 38.5 × 11 × 9.5 cm.
Fondation Arp, Clamart.

94. *Ptolemy I*, 1953.
Bronze, 103 × 53 × 43 cm.
Fondation Arp, Clamart.

92

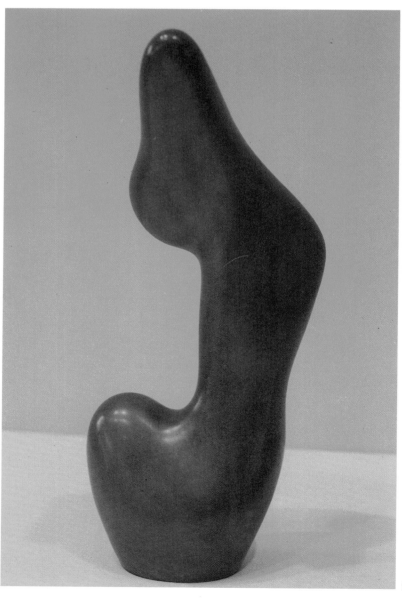

93

95. *Meudon Venus*, 1956.
Bronze, 158 × 40 × 40 cm.
Musée Louisiana.

95

96

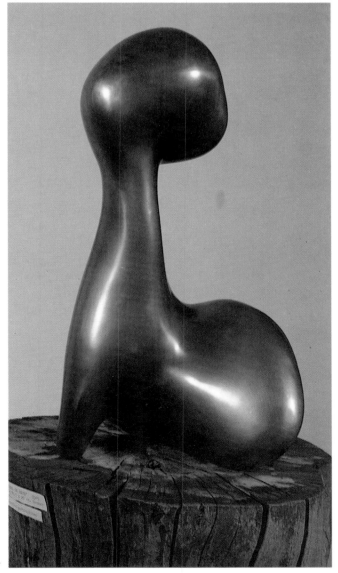

96. *Configurations with Snake Movements*, 1955.
Bronze, 21 × 34 × 29 cm.
Fondation Arp, Clamart.

97. *Animal Conscious of Its Beauty*, 1957.
Bronze, 51 × 80 × 38.5 cm.
Musée National d'Art Moderne, Paris.

97

98 & 99. *Daphne II*, 1958-60.
Bronze, 155 × 42 × 42 cm.
Fondation Arp, Clamart.

100. *Meudon Knot*, 1958.
Crystal, 46 × 58 × 34.5 cm.
Private Collection, Locarno.

98

99

101. *Ptolemy II*, 1958.
Bronze, 100 × 52 × 48 cm.
Fondation Arp, Clamart.

101

102. *Little Theater*, 1959.
Bronze, 105 × 67 × 8 cm.
Galerie Denise René.

103. *Torso-Bundle*, 1958.
Plaster, 67 × 37 × 28.5 cm.
Fondation Arp, Clamart.

104. *Leaf at Rest*, 1959.
Bronze, 120 × 192 × 44 cm.
Town of Marl, Federal Republic of Germany.

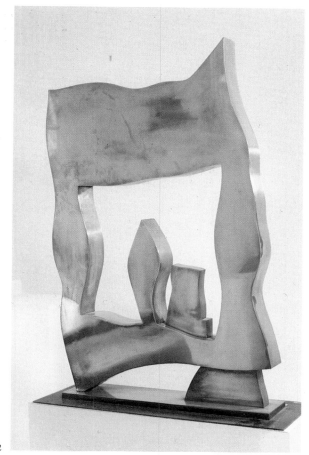

102

103

104

105

106

107

109

109. *Dancing Ceremony*, 1960.
Bronze, 118×76×10.5 cm.
Fondation Arp, Clamart.

110. *Undulating Threshold*, 1960.
Bronze, 46×65×10.5 cm.
Galerie Denise René.

111. *Ptolemy III*, 1961.
Bronze, 202.5×112×79 cm.
Beyeler Collection, Basel.

112. *Pointing at Clouds*, 1961.
Marble, 41 × 22 × 17 cm.
Fondation Arp, Clamart.

113. *Drawer Head*, 1960.
Bronze, 44 × 29 × 14 cm.
Fondation Arp-S. Taeuber, Rolandseck.

114. *Nude with Buds*, 1961.
Bronze, 188 × 32 × 30.5 cm.
Galerie Denise René.

115. *Demeter's Doll*, 1961.
Bronze, 83 × 29.5 × 29.5 cm.
Ionel Jianou Collection, Clamart.

112

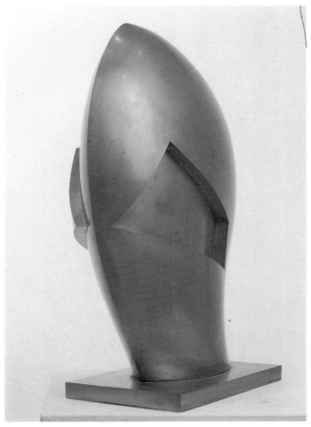

113

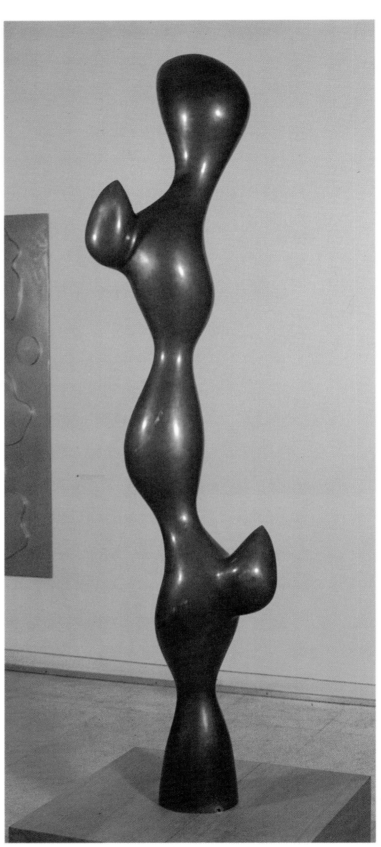

114

88

115

116. *Wall Relief*, 1961.
Concrete.
Gewerbeschule, Basel.

116

117. *Forest-Wheel I*, 1961.
Granite, 90×82×20 cm.
Arp Collection, Solduno.

118. *Forest-Wheel IV*, 1961.
Granite, 93.5×92×18 cm.
Modern Art Museum, Locarno.

117

118

91

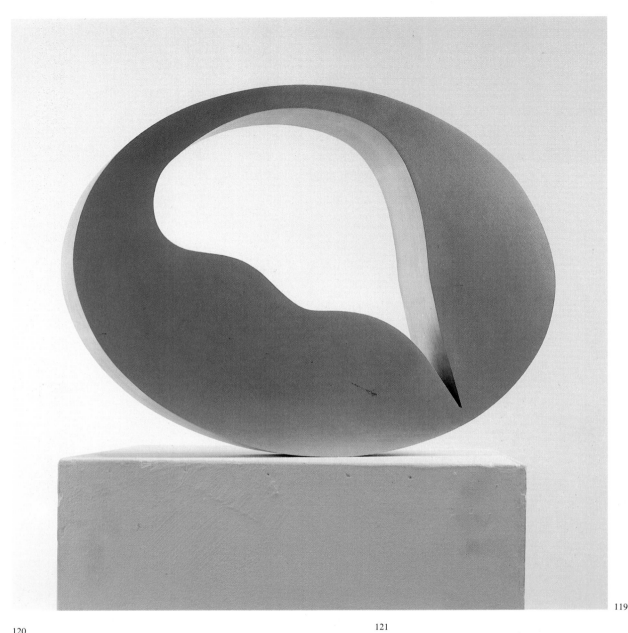

119

120

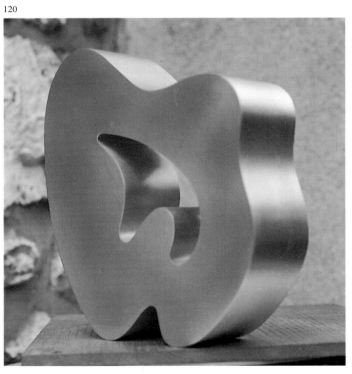

121

119. *Banner-Wheel*, 1962.
Duralumin, 30 × 39 × 6 cm.
Galerie Denise René.

120. *Oriforme*, 1962.
Duralumin, 24 × 21.5 × 6 cm.
Fondation Arp, Clamart.

121. *Man Tower Triers*, 1961.
Bronze, 11 × 9.5 × 5.5 cm.
Fondation Arp, Clamart.

122. *Galaxy Tear*, 1962.
Bronze, 68 × 60 × 50 cm.
Fondation Arp, Clamart.

122

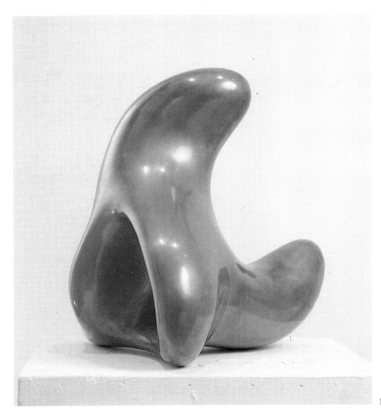

123

123. *Cloud Animal*, 1961.
Bronze, 26 × 33 × 31 cm.
Fondation Arp-S. Taeuber, Rolandseck.

124. *Gur*, 1963.
Bronze, 97 × 23.5 × 33 cm.
Fondation Arp, Clamart.

125. *The Outskirt Saint*, 1963.
Bronze, 74 × 36.5 × 21.5 cm.
Fondation Arp, Clamart.

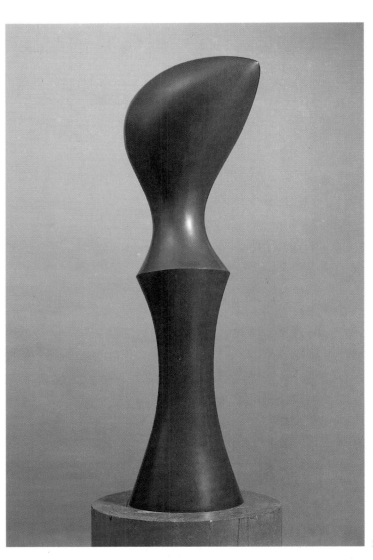

124

126. *Two Goblets*, 1963-64.
Unpublished plaster, 82.5 × 37 × 40 cm.
Fondation Arp, Clamart.

127. *Leaf-Torso*, 1963.
Bronze, 210 × 50 × 35 cm.
Fondation Arp-S. Taeuber, Rolandseck.

128. *Vase-Torso*, 1963.
Marble, 79 × 15 × 9 cm.
Galerie Denise René.

126

127

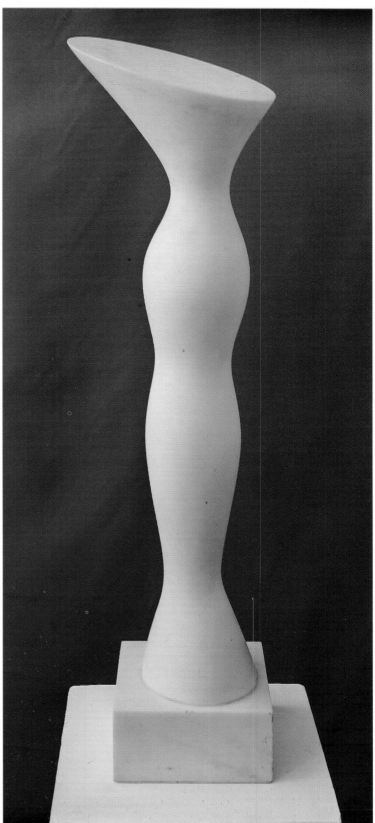

128

129. *Idol*, 1964.
Bronze, 63.5×22×9.5 cm.
Fondation Arp, Clamart.

129

130. *Scanning the Horizon*, 1964.
Bronze, 110×45×35 cm.
Brookstreet Gallery, London.

131. *Aggressive Fruit*, 1965.
Bronze, 86.5×52×22.5 cm.
Fondation Arp, Clamart.

130

131

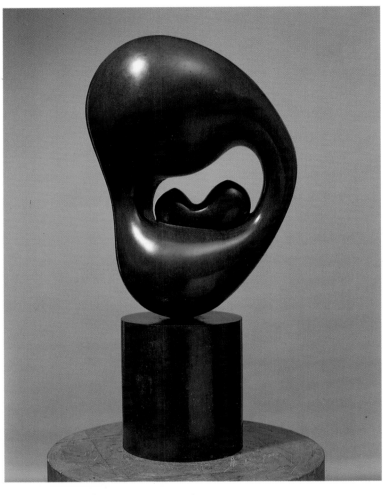

132. *Delightful Nest*, 1965.
Bronze, 62.5 × 30 × 18 cm.
Fondation Arp, Clamart.

133. *Eye of the Tower*, 1965.
Marble, 57 × 47.5 × 46 cm.
Arp Estate, Locarno.

134. *Yawning Shell*, 1965.
Bronze, 15.5 × 22 × 15 cm.
Fondation Arp-S. Taeuber, Rolandseck.

135. *Star Amphora*, 1965.
Bronze, 130 × 50 × 38 cm.
Fondation Arp, Clamart.

132

133

134

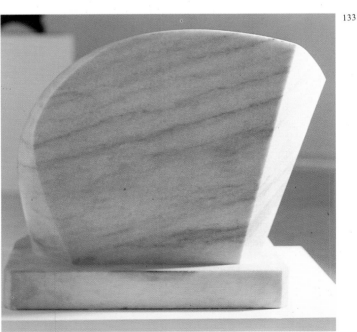

136. *Inverted Columns*, 1965.
Duralumin, 48 × 24 × 14 cm.
Galerie Denise René.

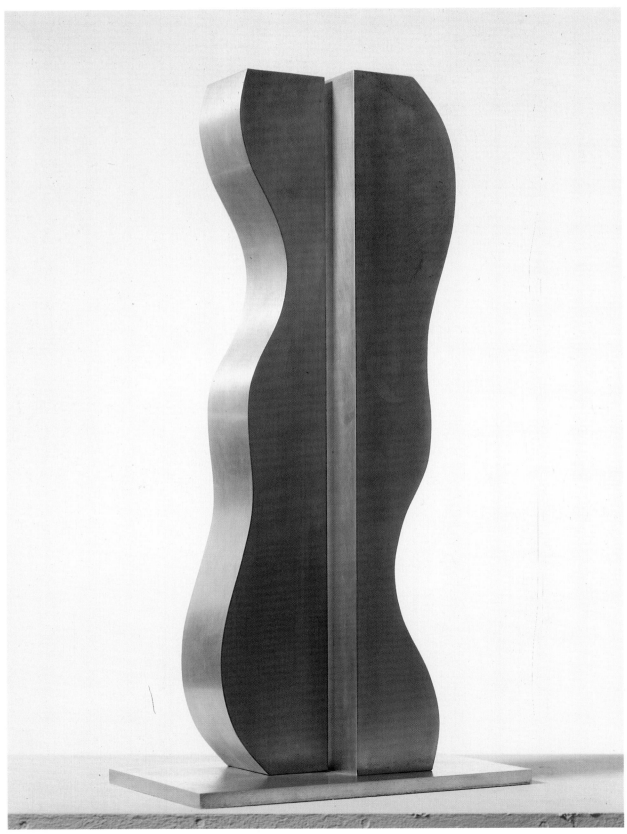

136

137

137. *Abstract Composition*, 1915.
Painted wood, 74.5×90.5 cm.
Museum of Contemporary Art, Theran.

138. *Hammer-Flower*, 1916.
Painted wood, 62 × 50 cm.
François Arp Collection, Paris.

139. *Navel-Torso*, 1915.
Natural wood, 26 × 17 cm.
Fondation Arp, Clamart.

140. *Forest*, 1916-17.
Painted wood, 32 × 19.5 × 7.5 cm.
Fondation Arp, Clamart.

138

139

140

141. *Bird Mask*, 1918.
Natural wood, 19×23 cm.
Fondation Arp, Clamart.

142. *DA Kit*, 1920.
Painted wood, 39×27.5 cm.
Formerly in the Tzara Collection.

141

142

143

143. *Shirt Front and Fork*, 1922-27.
Painted wood, 39 × 37 cm.
Mazoh & Co., New York.

144. *Infinitely Bound Form*, 1923.
Painted wood, 53 × 38.5 cm.
Fondation Arp, Clamart.

145. *Clock*, 1924.
Painted wood, diameter 54 cm.
M. Arp-Hagenbach Collection.

146. *Torsos Holding a Horse's Head by the Bridle*, 1925.
Wood on cardboard, 77 × 28 cm.
Private Collection.

147. *Torso with Flower Head*, 1924.
Painted wood, 87 × 72 cm.
Fondation Arp, Clamart.

144

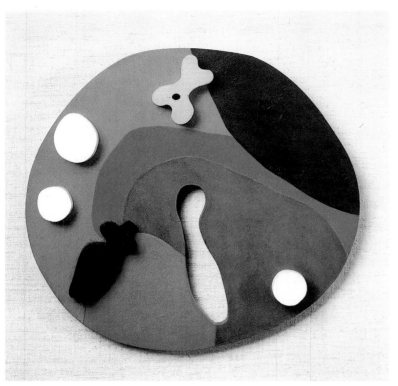

145

146

147

107

148. *Head with Bristling Moustache*, 1926.
Painted wood, 48 × 55.5 cm.
Fondation Arp, Clamart.

149. *Bird's Head*, 1924-25.
Painted wood, 29 × 21 cm.
Yale University Art Gallery.

150. *Navel Bottle (Navel-Torso)*, 1926.
Painted wood, 38.3 × 30 cm.
François Arp Collection, Paris.

151. *Untitled*, 1926.
Painted wood, 27 × 21 cm.
E. Jaguer Collection, Paris.

148

149

150

151

152. *Navel Bottles*, 1926.
Painted wood, 62.5 × 46 cm.
François Arp Collection, Paris.

152

153

154

153. *Lips and Hand Glass*, 1927.
Painted wood, 58 × 100 cm.
Private collection, Brussels.

154. *Spoon and Navels*, 1928.
Painted wood, 70.5 × 51 cm.
François Arp Collection, Paris.

155. *Shell Head and Tie*, 1928.
Natural wood, 25.7 × 33.5 cm.
A. Juda Gallery, London.

156. *Constellation of White Forms on Grey
Background*, 1929.
Painted wood, 72 × 87 cm.
Kunstmuseum, Duisburg.

162

163

164

165

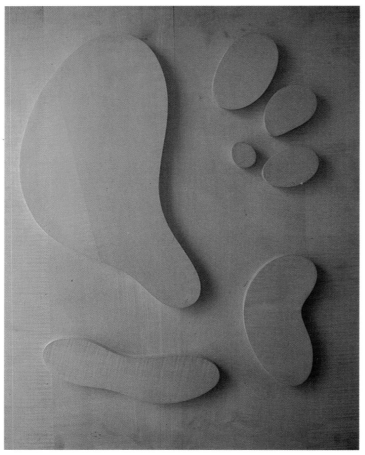

166

167

165. *Star Seed*, 1949.
Painted wood, 44.5 × 62 cm.
A. Juda Gallery, London.

166. *Constellation*, 1953.
Natural wood, 75 × 59 cm.
Fondation Arp-S. Taeuber, Rolandseck.

167. *Profile*, 1955.
Natural wood, 24 × 16.5 cm.
Van Doesburg Estate, The Hague.

168. *Bird of Ill Omen*, 1951.
Painted wood, 29 × 34.5 cm.
Fondation Arp, Clamart.

169. *Constellation*, 1951-52.
Painted wood, 29 × 34.5 cm.
Fondation Arp, Clamart.

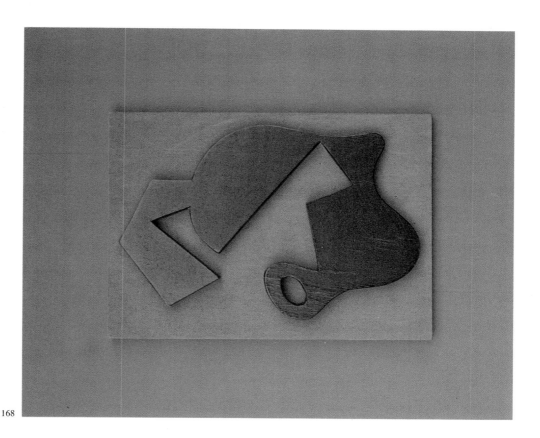

168

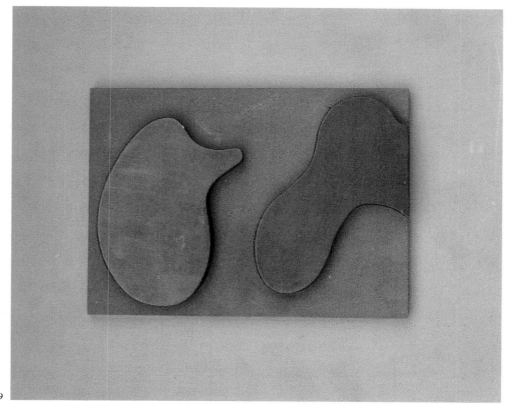

169

170. *Spider*, 1958.
Bronze, 36 × 45 cm.
Fondation Arp-S. Taeuber, Rolandseck.

171. *Glove*, 1958.
Bronze, 32 × 48 cm.
Arp Estate, Switzerland.

170

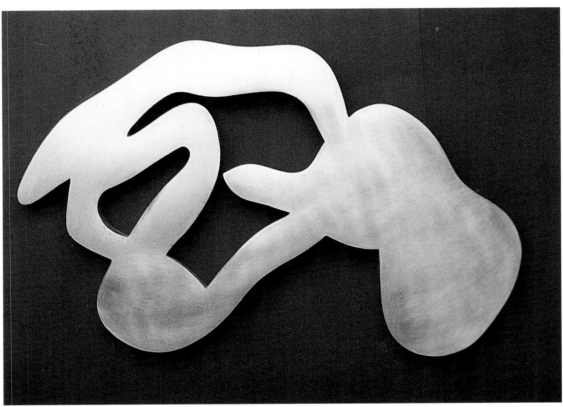

171

172. *Spiny-Handled Heart*, 1958.
Bronze, 42×26 cm.
Arp Estate, Switzerland.

172

173

173. *Echo-Mirror*, 1958.
Painted wood, 41.5×31 cm.
Galerie Denise René.

174. *Floral*, 1959.
Scooped-out painted wood, 57.5×48 cm.
Fondation Arp, Clamart.

174

175. *Page from a Floral Book*, 1960.
Cardboard, 50×65 cm.
Galerie Denise René.

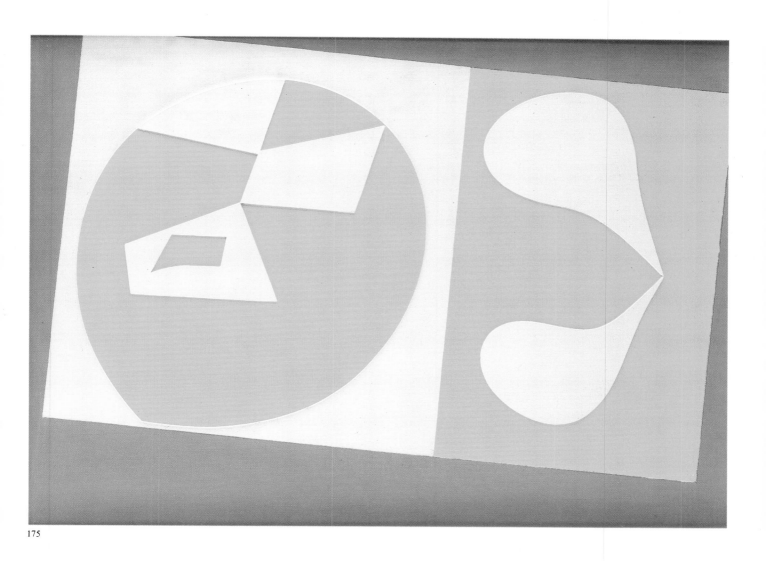

175

176. *Elevation of Figure I (Concrete Relief F)*, 1961.
Duralumin, 150 × 35.5 cm.
Fondation Arp, Clamart.

177. *Bird — Mask*, 1966.
Gilded metal, multiple, 20 × 15 cm.

178. *Composition in a Circle*, 1963.
Duralumin and bronze, 26 × 26 cm.
Fondation Arp, Clamart.

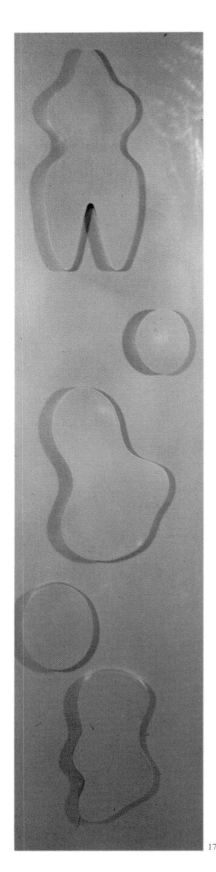

176

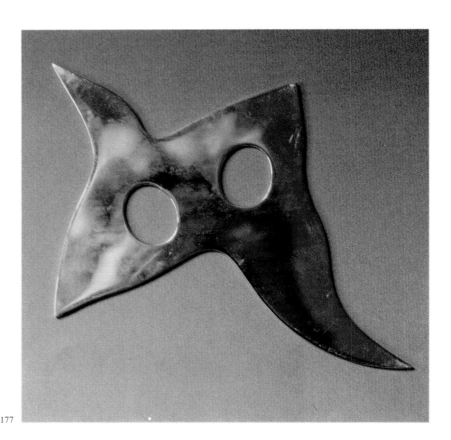

177

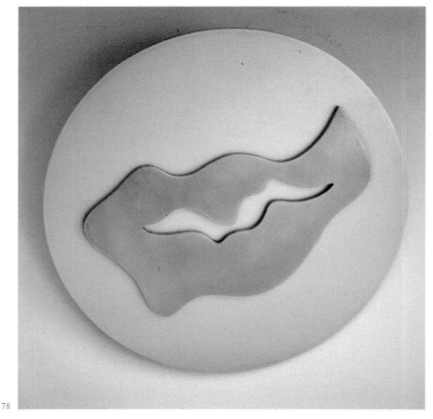

178

179. *The Little Prince*, 1962.
Painted wood, 57 × 20 cm.
Fondation Arp, Clamart.

180. *Hero — Top*, 1963.
Painted wood, 98 × 53 cm.
Fondation Arp, Clamart.

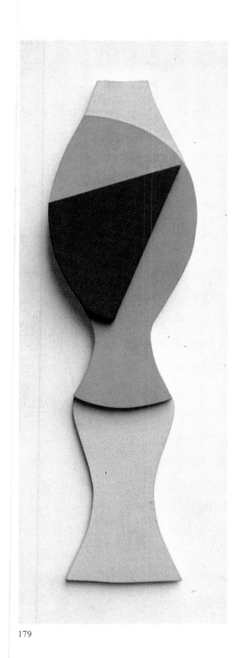

179

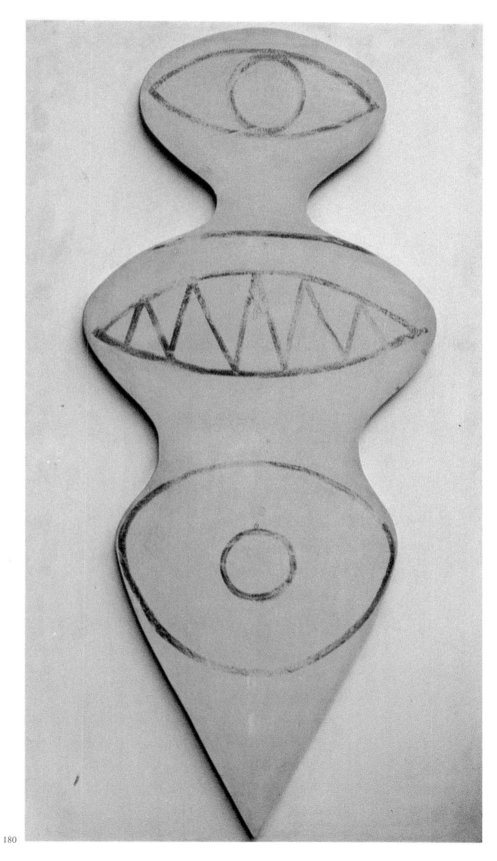

180

181. *Constellation on Two Levels*, 1964.
Natural wood, 43.5 × 42 cm.
Fondation Arp, Clamart.

182. *Antipodes of the Coin I*, 1964.
Painted wood, 34 × 36 cm.
Fondation Arp, Clamart.

183. *Transformation of a Head with Green Nose*, 1964.
Painted wood, 42 × 47 × 9 cm.
Fondation Arp, Clamart.

181

182

183

184. *Antipodes of the Coin II*, 1965.
Painted wood, 33 × 42 cm.
Chalette Gallery, New York.

184

LIST OF ILLUSTRATIONS

SCULPTURES

63. The garden at Meudon-Clamart; in the background, Arp's studio. From left to right: *The Outskirt Saint; Bird Skeleton; Demeter; Classical Sculpture.*

64. *Fruit of a Hand*, 1927-28.
Painted wood, 55 × 88 × 20 cm.
Kunsthaus, Zurich.
Photograph: G. Mahn.

65. *Amphora* (with Sophie Taeuber), 1917.
Painted wood.
Height: 30 cm.
Fondation Arp, Clamart.
Photograph: G. Ströh.

66. *Kaspar*, 1930.
Bronze, 50 × 28 × 19 cm.
Chalette Collection, New York.

67. *One Large and Two Small*, 1931.
Painted wood, 63 × 45 cm.
Fondation Arp, Clamart.
Photograph: G. Ströh.

68. *Shell Head*, 1933.
Bronze, 20 × 25 × 18.5 cm.
Fondation Arp-S. Taeuber, Rolandseck.
Photograph: G. Ströh.

69. *Pagoda Fruit*, 1934.
Cement, 23 × 33 × 38 cm.
Fondation Arp, Clamart.
Photograph: G. Ströh.

70. *Human Concretion on Goblet*, 1935.
Bronze, 47 × 74 × 45.5 cm.
Fondation Arp, Clamart.

71. *Crown of Buds*, 1936.
Bronze, 52 × 42.5 × 42 cm.
Fondation Arp, Clamart.

72 & 73. *Moon Fruit*, 1936.
Stone, 110 × 150 × 100 cm.
Fondation Arp, Clamart.
Photograph: G. Mahn.

74 & 75. *Seated*, 1937.
Bronze, 33 × 40 × 20 cm.
Fondation Arp, Clamart.
Photograph: G. Mahn.

76. *Pre-Adamite Fruit*, 1938.
Bronze, 29.5 × 23.5 × 17 cm.
Fondation Arp, Clamart.
Photograph: G. Ströh.

77. *Dreaming*, 1937.
Bronze, 37 × 20 × 21 cm.
Fondation Arp, Clamart.
Photograph: G. Ströh.

78. *Homage to Rodin*, 1938-65.
Plaster, 27 × 22 × 11.5 cm.
Fondation Arp, Clamart.
Photograph: G. Ströh.

79. *Owl Dream*, 1937-38.
Plaster, 26 × 15 × 13 cm.
Fondation Arp, Clamart.
Photograph: G. Ströh.

80. *Milestone* (with Sophie Taeuber), 1938.
Wood, 60 × 25 × 36 cm.
Fondation Arp, Clamart.
Photograph: G. Ströh.

81. *Mediterranean Sculpture I*, 1941.
Bronze, 38 × 27 × 16.5 cm.
Fondation Arp, Clamart.
Photograph: G. Ströh.

82. *Mediterranean Group*, 1941-42.
Bronze, 21 × 35 × 17.5 cm.
Fondation Arp, Clamart.
Photograph: G. Ströh.

83. *Geometrical-Ageometrical*, 1942.
Bronze, 30 × 28.5 × 16.5 cm.
Fondation Arp, Clamart.
Photograph: G. Ströh.

84. *Superimposed Goblets*, 1947.
Bronze, 97 × 45 × 47 cm.
Fondation Arp, Clamart.
Photograph: G. Ströh.

85. *Bird Skeleton*, 1947.
Bronze, 108 × 57 × 57 cm.
Fondation Arp, Clamart.
Photograph: G. Ströh.

86. Another view of the same.
Photograph: B. Weill.

87. *Impish Shape*, 1949.
Bronze, 39 × 15 × 18 cm.
Fondation Arp, Clamart.
Photograph: G. Ströh.

88 & 89. *Frond*, 1950.
Stone, 30 × 20.5 × 17.5 cm.
Fondation Arp, Clamart.

90. *Pistil*, 1950.
Cement, 88 × 40 × 36 cm.
Fondation Arp, Clamart.

91. *Mythical Figure*, 1950.
Bronze, 113 × 38.5 × 35 cm.
Fondation Arp, Clamart.
Photograph: G. Ströh.

92. *Evocation of a Human, Moon-like, Ghostly Form*, 1950.
Bronze, 28 × 22.5 × 17 cm.
Fondation Arp, Clamart.
Photograph: G. Ströh.

93. *Howl*, 1951.
Bronze, 38.5 × 11 × 9.5 cm.
Fondation Arp, Clamart.
Photograph: G. Ströh.

94. *Ptolemy I*, 1953.
Bronze, 103 × 53 × 43 cm.
Fondation Arp, Clamart.
Photograph: B. Weill.

95. *Meudon Venus*, 1956.
Bronze, 158 × 40 × 40 cm.
Musée Louisiana.
Photograph: G. Ströh.

96. *Configurations with Snake Movements*, 1955.
Bronze, 21 × 34 × 29 cm.
Fondation Arp, Clamart.
Photograph: G. Ströh.

97. *Animal Conscious of Its Beauty*, 1957.
Bronze, 51 × 80 × 38.5 cm.
Musée National d'Art Moderne, Paris.

98. & 99. *Daphne II*, 1958-60.
Bronze, 155 × 42 × 42 cm.
Fondation Arp, Clamart.
Photograph: G. Mahn.

100. *Meudon Knot*, 1958.
Crystal, 46 × 58 × 34.5 cm.
Private Collection, Locarno.

101. *Ptolemy II*, 1958.
Bronze, 100 × 52 × 48 cm.
Fondation Arp, Clamart.
Photograph: G. Mahn.

102. *Little Theater*, 1959.
Bronze, 105 × 67 × 8 cm.
Galerie Denise René.

103. *Torso-Bundle*, 1958.
Plaster, 67 × 37 × 28.5 cm.
Fondation Arp, Clamart.
Photograph: G. Ströh.

104. *Leaf at Rest*, 1959.
Bronze, 120 × 192 × 44 cm.
Town of Marl, Federal Republic of Germany.
Photograph: G. Ströh.

105. *Star*, 1960.
Bronze, 84.5 × 68 × 43.5 cm.
On the artist's grave, Locarno.
Photograph: G. Ströh.

106. *Torso-Fruit*, 1960.
Bronze, 75 × 29 × 30 cm.
Marcel-Jean Collection.
Photograph: G. Ströh.

107. *Initial of a Bronze Leaf*, 1960.
Bronze, 147 × 165 × 21 cm.
Galerie Denise René.

108. View of the same in another position.

109. *Dancing Ceremony*, 1960.
Bronze, 118 × 76 × 10.5 cm.
Fondation Arp, Clamart.

110. *Undulating Threshold*, 1960.
Bronze, 46 × 65 × 10.5 cm.
Galerie Denise René.

111. *Ptolemy III*, 1961.
Bronze, 202.5 × 112 × 79 cm.
Beyeler Collection, Basel.
Photograph: G. Ströh.

112. *Pointing at Clouds*, 1961.
Marble, 41 × 22 × 17 cm.
Fondation Arp, Clamart.
Photograph: G. Ströh.

113. *Drawer Head*, 1960.
Bronze, 44 × 29 × 14 cm.
Fondation Arp-S. Taeuber, Rolandseck.

114. *Nude with Buds*, 1961.
Bronze, 188 × 32 × 30.5 cm.
Galerie Denise René.

115. *Demeter's Doll*, 1961.
Bronze, 83 × 29.5 × 29.5 cm.
Ionel Jianou Collection, Clamart.

116. *Wall Relief*, 1961.
Concrete.
Gewerbeschule, Basel.

117. *Forest-Wheel I*, 1961.
Granite, 90 × 82 × 20 cm.
Arp Collection, Solduno.
Photograph: G. Ströh.

118. *Forest-Wheel IV*, 1961.
Granite, 93.5 × 92 × 18 cm.
Modern Art Museum, Locarno.
Photograph: G. Ströh.

119. *Banner-Wheel*, 1962.
Duralumin, 30 × 39 × 6 cm.
Galerie Denise René.
Photograph: Dumage.

120. *Oriforme*, 1962.
Duralumin, 24 × 21.5 × 6 cm.
Fondation Arp, Clamart.
Photograph: G. Ströh.

121. *Man Tower Triers*, 1961.
Bronze, 11 × 9.5 × 5.5 cm.
Fondation Arp, Clamart.
Photograph: G. Ströh.

122. *Galaxy Tear*, 1962.
Bronze, 68 × 60 × 50 cm.
Fondation Arp, Clamart.

123. *Cloud Animal*, 1961.
Bronze, 26 × 33 × 31 cm.
Fondation Arp-S. Taeuber, Rolandseck.

124. *Gur*, 1963.
Bronze, 97 × 23.5 × 33 cm.
Fondation Arp, Clamart.

125. *The Outskirt Saint*, 1963.
Bronze, 74 × 36.5 × 21.5 cm.
Fondation Arp, Clamart.
Photograph: B. Weill.

126. *Two Goblets*, 1963-64.
Unpublished plaster, 82.5 × 37 × 40 cm.
Fondation Arp, Clamart.

127. *Leaf-Torso*, 1963.
Bronze, 210 × 50 × 35 cm.
Fondation Arp-S. Taeuber, Rolandseck.

128. *Vase-Torso*, 1963.
Marble, 79 × 15 × 9 cm.
Galerie Denise René.

129. *Idol*, 1964.
Bronze, 63.5 × 22 × 9.5 cm.
Fondation Arp, Clamart.
Photograph: G. Ströh.

130. *Scanning the Horizon*, 1964.
Bronze, 110 × 45 × 35 cm.
Brookstreet Gallery, London.

131. *Aggressive Fruit*, 1965.
Bronze, 86.5 × 52 × 22.5 cm.
Fondation Arp, Clamart.

132. *Delightful Nest*, 1965.
Bronze, 62.5 × 30 × 18 cm.
Fondation Arp, Clamart.
Photograph: B. Weill.

133. *Eye of the Tower*, 1965.
Marble, 57 × 47.5 × 46 cm.
Arp Estate, Locarno.

134. *Yawning Shell*, 1965.
Bronze, 15.5 × 22 × 15 cm.
Fondation Arp-S. Taeuber, Rolandseck.

135. *Star Amphora*, 1965.
Bronze, 130 × 50 × 38 cm.
Fondation Arp, Clamart.
Photograph: G. Ströh.

136. *Inverted Columns*, 1965.
Duralumin, 48 × 24 × 14 cm.
Galerie Denise René.

RELIEFS

137. *Abstract Composition*, 1915.
Painted wood, 74.5 × 90.5 cm.
Museum of Contemporary Art, Theran.

138. *Hammer-Flower*, 1916.
Painted wood, 62 × 50 cm.
François Arp Collection, Paris.

139. *Navel-Torso*, 1915.
Natural wood, 26 × 17 cm.
Fondation Arp, Clamart.

140. *Forest*, 1916-17.
Painted wood, 32 × 19.5 × 7.5 cm.
Fondation Arp, Clamart.
Photograph: G. Ströh.

141. *Bird Mask*, 1918.
Natural wood, 19 × 23 cm.
Fondation Arp, Clamart.
Photograph: G. Ströh.

142. *DA Kit*, 1920.
Painted wood, 39 × 27.5 cm.
Formerly in the Tzara Collection.
Photograph: G. Ströh.

143. *Shirt Front and Fork*, 1922-27.
Painted wood, 39 × 37 cm.
Mazoh & Co., New York.
Photograph: G. Ströh.

144. *Infinitely Bound Form*, 1923.
Painted wood, 53 × 38.5 cm.
Fondation Arp, Clamart.
Photograph: G. Ströh.

145. *Clock*, 1924.
Painted wood, diameter 54 cm.
M. Arp-Hagenbach Collection.
Photograph: G. Ströh.

146. *Torsos Holding a Horse's Head by the Bridle*, 1925.
Wood on cardboard, 77 × 28 cm.
Private Collection.
Photograph: G. Ströh.

147. *Torso with Flower Head*, 1924.
Painted wood, 87 × 72 cm.
Fondation Arp, Clamart.
Photograph: G. Ströh.

148. *Head with Bristling Moustache*, 1926.
Painted wood, 48 × 55.5 cm.
Fondation Arp, Clamart.
Photograph: G. Ströh.

149. *Bird's Head*, 1924-25.
Painted wood, 29 × 21 cm.
Yale University Art Gallery.
Photograph: G. Ströh.

150. *Navel Bottle (Navel-Torso)*, 1926.
Painted wood, 38.3 × 30 cm.
François Arp Collection, Paris.
Photograph: G. Mahn.

151. *Untitled*, 1926.
Painted wood, 27 × 21 cm.
E. Jaguer Collection, Paris.
Photograph: G. Mahn.

152. *Navel Bottles*, 1926.
Painted wood, 62.5 × 46 cm.
François Arp Collection, Paris.
Photograph: G. Mahn.

153. *Lips and Hand Glass*, 1927.
Painted wood, 58 × 100 cm.
Private collection, Brussels.

154. *Spoon and Navels*, 1928.
Painted wood, 70.5 × 51 cm.
François Arp Collection, Paris.
Photograph: G. Mahn.

155. *Shell Head and Tie*, 1928.
Natural wood, 25.7 × 33.5 cm.
A. Juda Gallery, London.
Photograph: G. Mahn.

156. *Constellation of White Forms on Grey Background*, 1929.
Painted wood, 72 × 87 cm.
Kunstmuseum, Duisburg.
Photograph: G. Ströh.

157. *Randomly Placed Objects*, 1931.
Painted wood, 25.5 × 28 cm.
Fondation Arp, Clamart.
Photograph: G. Ströh.

158. *Constellation*, 1938-39.
Natural wood, 50.2 × 50.2 cm.
Museum of Modern Art, New York.

159, 162 & 163. *Triptych — Three Constellations with the Same Shape*, 1942.
91 × 71 cm. each.
Deutsche Bank Collection, Düsseldorf.

160. *Constellation*, 1938.
Bronze, 38 × 33 × 10 cm.
Galerie Denise René.

161. *Three Prints*, 1941.
Marble, 25 × 17 cm.
Fondation Arp, Clamart.
Photograph: G. Ströh.

164. *Part of an Infinity*, 1941.
Marble, 14 × 21 cm.
Fondation Arp, Clamart.
Photograph: G. Ströh.

165. *Star Seed*, 1949.
Painted wood, 44.5 × 62 cm.
A. Juda Gallery, London.
Photograph: G. Mahn.

166. *Constellation*, 1953.
Natural wood, 75 × 59 cm.
Fondation Arp-S. Taeuber, Rolandseck.

167. *Profile*, 1955.
Natural wood, 24 × 16.5 cm.
Van Doesburg Estate, The Hague.
Photograph: G. Mahn.

168. *Bird of Ill Omen*, 1951.
Painted wood, 29 × 34.5 cm.
Fondation Arp, Clamart.
Photograph: G. Ströh.

169. *Constellation*, 1951-52.
Painted wood, 29 × 34.5 cm.
Fondation Arp, Clamart.
Photograph: G. Ströh.

170. *Spider*, 1958.
Bronze, 36 × 45 cm.
Fondation Arp-S. Taeuber, Rolandseck.
Photograph: G. Ströh.

171. *Glove*, 1958.
Bronze, 32 × 48 cm.
Arp Estate, Switzerland.
Photograph: G. Ströh.

172. *Spiny-Handled Heart*, 1958.
Bronze, 42 × 26 cm.
Arp Estate, Switzerland.
Photograph: Dumage.

173. *Echo-Mirror*, 1958.
Painted wood, 41.5 × 31 cm.
Galerie Denise René.

174. *Floral*, 1959.
Scooped-out painted wood, 57.5 × 48 cm.
Fondation Arp, Clamart.
Photograph: G. Ströh.

175. *Page from a Floral Book*, 1960.
Cardboard, 50 × 65 cm.
Galerie Denise René.

176. *Elevation of Figure I (Concrete Relief F)*, 1961.
Duralumin, 150 × 35.5 cm.
Fondation Arp, Clamart.

177. *Bird — Mask*, 1966.
Gilded metal, multiple, 20 × 15 cm.
Photograph: G. Ströh.

178. *Composition in a Circle*, 1963.
Duralumin and bronze, 26 × 26 cm.
Fondation Arp, Clamart.

179. *The Little Prince*, 1962.
Painted wood, 57 × 20 cm.
Fondation Arp, Clamart.
Photograph: G. Ströh.

180. *Hero — Top*, 1963.
Painted wood, 98 × 53 cm.
Fondation Arp, Clamart.
Photograph: G. Ströh.

181. *Constellation on Two Levels*, 1964.
Natural wood, 43.5 × 42 cm.
Fondation Arp, Clamart.
Photograph: G. Ströh.

182. *Antipodes of the Coin I*, 1964.
Painted wood, 34 × 36 cm.
Fondation Arp, Clamart.

183. *Transformation of a Head with Green Nose*, 1964.
Painted wood, 42 × 47 × 9 cm.
Fondation Arp, Clamart.
Photograph: G. Ströh.

184. *Antipodes of the Coin II*, 1965.
Painted wood, 33 × 42 cm.
Chalette Gallery, New York.
Photograph: B. Weill.